HD39.5 .A55 2008
0134110392336
Anklesaria, Jimmy.

Supply chain cost
   management : the A
      c2008.

D0329013

2007 11 16

DISCARD

ply chain practitioners provides invaluable advice to anyone serious about supply collaboration and genuine cost removal."

—Joe Sandor, Hoagland-Metzler Endowed Professor of Practice in Supply Management,
The Eli Broad Graduate School of Business

"AIM & DRIVE is one of the main processes we have implemented at Nokia Sourcing and Procurement in the scope of Material Cost Leadership. The systematic approach of this methodology and the analysis of the key cost drivers combined with our soft skills, reflected into our 'Passion and Trust' values, have produced a clear advantage for Nokia at the system level. We have now fully deployed AIM & DRIVE at Nokia for all component solutions. AIM & DRIVE is also playing a major role in our overall cooperation and collaboration with our suppliers' network in a very positive partnership spirit which is the foundation of our strategy."

—Jean-Francois Baril, Senior Vice President,
Sourcing and Procurement, Nokia Corporation

"Anklesaria's AIM & DRIVE process helped to open the eyes of procurement professionals and generated value-added and breakthrough ideas at Deutsche Telekom, which we needed to improve the bottom line."

—Hans Heith, Chief Procurement Officer, Deutsche Telekom

"I have led the execution of the AIM & DRIVE process in two major corporations (Texas Instruments and Motorola) for over thirteen years. This process has yielded greater cost reduction in the supply chain than any other method I have seen used. It is also one of the best processes I know of to strengthen positive relationships with suppliers and has facilitated placing my company as the 'most favored customer' status with our suppliers."

—Ernie Cook, former Chief Procurement Officer,
Communications Computing Group, Motorola

"The teams trained in the AIM & DRIVE process delivered impressive results. It made no difference if the supplier was domestic or foreign or what the commodity was. If there was a cost removal opportunity it was uncovered and implemented. The process helped in overcoming internal barriers to implementation of change at both the customer and supplier."

—Phil Keller, former Manager Procurement Process, DuPont

"I have been engaged with Jimmy Anklesaria's AIM & DRIVE process over the past fifteen years with three top employers, soon to be four. The processes are outstanding! There is no other process that yields significant results every time regardless of the category. Every buyer, engineer, and strategic sourcing person must have these tools, processes, and methodologies in their intellectual toolbox."

—Tom Piersa, Vice President, Procurement & Supply Chain Management,
Allied Waste Industries (formerly with Eastman Kodak,
York International, and Maytag)

"I really believe in Jimmy Anklesaria's AIM & DRIVE process and have personally seen the results at IBM and Motorola. There are few processes that deliver a greater return on investment."

—Theresa Metty, Chairperson, Institute of Supply Management

Praise for *Supply Chain Cost Management*

"I have used the Anklesaria Cost Roadmap repeatedly over the last ten year three organizations, to great effect each time. We have been able to take milli dollars out of supply chain costs through knowing just how much there is th be avoided, either by identifying and jointly removing those costs that are no for us, or through helping suppliers take down their own cost base. The AIM & process is a great way to get a structured start, running the process in parall multiple suppliers."

> —Neil A. Deverill, Executive V.P. Procurement, Anglo Ameri(
> (formerly with Philips and Elec

"I have been personally involved with Anklesaria's AIM & DRIVE process ot past several years with two large employers. The process really works . . . ! I he to find any other methodology that provides a comparable return-on-investi

> —Steve Kesinger, Vice President, Procurement, Noi

"The AIM & DRIVE process is the facilitator of change. It gives focus and dii to the cost management effort. Senior management must have an understanc the process. They have to validate the targets and they have to make a comm to participate. With the above in place, AIM & DRIVE is a powerful tool tha\ goals and targets into real change, real bottom line impact. This is hard woi watching a team analyze, identify, learn, and structure options for action is 'neat stuff.' We looked at several tools to incorporate into our cost manag effort and chose AIM & DRIVE. The approach gave us the definitions, the wc pers, and the methodology to build the entire cost management program f marketing community. We didn't want to bring in a bunch of consultants, them our business, give them our data and processes, have them tell us wi know already, and then leave. AIM & DRIVE allows us to build an internal l edge base, points the process owners to the cost driver and promotes real, pern change."

> —Bob Quinn, Director of Business Operations, IBi

"I cannot believe that my teams and I have been using AIM & DRIVE techi since the very early 1990s! This is surely testimony to the value, durability relevance of AIM & DRIVE as a valuable way to collaboratively manage cost th the supply chain. Managing cost is always a sensitive issue with suppliers. Hoi the AIM & DRIVE process has continually proven its value by getting past the tions and getting to real cost management solutions that benefit both parties.

> —John Proverbs, Senior Director, Supply Chain, KLA-
> (formerly with IBM and Hewlett-Pa

"If you're interested in sustainable supply chain advantage along with (through cost reduction, read Jimmy Anklesaria's book. AIM & DRIVE is a prove robust process to systematically take cost out of your supply chain versus s transferring costs elsewhere. Jimmy's extensive experience with many premie

SUPPLY CHAIN
COST MANAGEMENT

GEORGIAN COLLEGE LIBRARY 2501   #41.95

250101

SUPPLY CHAIN
COST MANAGEMENT

The AIM & DRIVE® Process for
Achieving Extraordinary Results

Jimmy Anklesaria

**Library Commons
Georgian College
One Georgian Drive
Barrie, ON
L4M 3X9**

AMACOM
American Management Association
New York • Atlanta • Brussels • Chicago • Mexico City • San Francisco
Shanghai • Tokyo • Toronto • Washington, D.C.

Special discounts on bulk quantities of AMACOM books are
available to corporations, professional associations, and other
organizations. For details, contact Special Sales Department,
AMACOM, a division of American Management Association,
1601 Broadway, New York, NY 10019.
Tel: 212-903-8316. Fax: 212-903-8083.
E-mail: specialsls@amanet.org
Website: www. amacombooks.org/go/specialsales
To view all AMACOM titles go to: www.amacombooks.org

This publication is designed to provide accurate and authoritative
information in regard to the subject matter covered. It is sold with
the understanding that the publisher is not engaged in rendering
legal, accounting, or other professional service. If legal advice or
other expert assistance is required, the services of a competent
professional person should be sought.

AIM & DRIVE® is a registered trademark, and is used with
permission. Formula Based Costing™ is trademarked by Jimmy
Anklesaria and is used with permission.

Library of Congress Cataloging-in-Publication Data

Anklesaria, Jimmy.
    Supply chain cost management : the AIM & DRIVE process for achieving
extraordinary results / Jimmy Anklesaria.
       p.   cm.
    Includes bibliographical references and index.
    ISBN-13: 978–0-8144–7475–4
    ISBN-10: 0–8144–7475–6
    1. Industrial procurement—Cost effectiveness.   2. Industrial procurement—
Cost control.   3. Business logistics—Management.   I. Title.

HD39.5.A55   2008
658.7'2—dc22   2007013645

© 2008 Jimmy Anklesaria.
All rights reserved.
Printed in the United States of America.

This publication may not be reproduced,
stored in a retrieval system,
or transmitted in whole or in part,
in any form or by any means, electronic,
mechanical, photocopying, recording, or otherwise,
without the prior written permission of AMACOM,
a division of American Management Association,
1601 Broadway, New York, NY 10019.

Printing number

10   9   8   7   6   5   4   3   2   1

This book is dedicated to

my wife, Jennifer,

my son, Zubin,

daughters, Jasmine and Avi Lynn,

and

To my mentor and friend,

Gene Richter

(1937–2003)

Contents

Foreword

During my time at IBM and Motorola (1995–2005), there was one goal that drove us constantly: a *substantial* reduction in costs. The low-hanging fruit had been gathered, and we were still far from our targets. We needed something that would take us to the next level where our category teams could generate breakthrough ideas that would deliver a sustainable competitive advantage for the company. The answer was AIM & DRIVE. We successfully deployed it at both companies, and were able to take hundreds of millions of dollars out of supply chain costs. That alone would be reason enough for me to take the time to write this Foreword. But the magic of the AIM & DRIVE process is that while we were reducing costs, we were also improving key supplier and internal customer relationships.

I remember one particular instance where we were looking at ways to reduce the cost of our Marketing brochures and literature. We engaged our key supplier and our internal customers in an AIM & DRIVE session. The initial skepticism quickly faded as they grew to understand the AIM & DRIVE approach to taking cost out without ugly battles and heated debates. Together, we were able to dramatically streamline the process and save tens of millions of dollars. Not only was the supplier thrilled with the more efficient process, our internal customers were delighted that these savings were from genuine process improvements that did not compromise the effectiveness of the creative process.

In this book, Jimmy Anklesaria has provided a wonderful journey through the AIM & DRIVE process that is engaging and easy to read. Whether you are a C-level officer, senior manager, mid-level manager, or functional specialist, you're probably under pressure to reduce costs. This book will give you a proven methodology to leverage the collective intelligence of the extended enterprise (your customers and their customers, your suppliers and their suppliers), and generate substantial results. The examples and stories in each chapter are fun to read, and they bring all the concepts and steps to life. I suspect you will relate to most of them.

The first two chapters lay the groundwork for the process. They outline some of the problems with cost-management efforts today, demonstrate why collaboration is essential, and lay out a checklist for successfully deploying the process. The rest of the book provides a detailed walk-through of the AIM & DRIVE process. You will learn how to select the "right" team to develop strategies and agree on goals; identify critical costs; develop and define a comprehensive list of cost drivers; develop strategies that reduce, change, or eliminate activities; and much more.

While all of this sounds extremely complex, the beauty of AIM & DRIVE is its *lack* of complexity. It is not burdened with complicated and time-consuming numerical and statistical algorithms. It facilitates the creation of breakthrough ideas quickly and effectively, and can be used by everyone across the enterprise. As you go through the eight steps of the process in this book, that fact will become abundantly clear.

I've personally seen the process deliver great results. It takes us far beyond the traditional world of cost accounting, cost modeling, and price negotiation. It is much more powerful . . . and it works. Watching my teams first-hand was truly exciting. One team after another came to understand the true benefits of the AIM & DRIVE process. To see them working closely with our key suppliers and internal customers to achieve huge sustainable cost reductions, all the while improving relationships, was truly amazing. You're in for a real treat!

Theresa Metty
Board Chair (2005–2007), Institute of Supply Management;
Former Chief Procurement Officer, Motorola;
Former VP-Procurement, IBM

Preface

How many times have you wanted to take your company's costs down by 5 percent, 10 percent, even 50 percent? Cost management is the key to profitability, and cost management is the key to successful supply networks. Take the money you save, and use it to build a new plant, or develop a new product, or make your stockholders rich! The point is, even if you don't know how much your company is spending in purchased materials and labor and logistics—and believe it or not, most companies, even some Best Practice leaders, don't—you will find significant savings, just exactly the way we did at Honda, TRW, Delphi, and John Deere, by managing on your operation's *true* costs.

The real power of cost management is to know from the creation of a new part, product, or service what the true purchased costs are—not the costs developed after-the-fact simply from prices set by the marketplace or bids from a variety of suppliers. These "costs" most likely will not represent or even come close to the optimum product cost developed by using the cost management concepts in this book.

This cost management concept is the most powerful supply management concept today. The AIM & DRIVE process takes you far beyond the benefits of negotiated savings and facilitates breakthrough cost solutions. Genuine cost management is different from cost cutting. Anyone can do that. However, the best-in-class companies engage their supply base in tough negotiations, set aggressive stretch targets, and use a defined process of managing supply chain costs.

This kind of cost management is the key reason that Toyota, Honda, and Nissan are so competitive compared to today's American automotive "Big Three." Although most people want to attribute Toyota, Honda, and Nissan's (JB3) success to "lean manufacturing techniques" in their own manufacturing assembly operations, that is really only somewhat true because *75 to 80 percent of the cost of a car is purchased cost*, compared to 20 percent in-house cost. The JB3s often say, "How goes Purchasing is how goes the company."

With 75 to 80 percent of the vehicle cost controlled by Purchasing, it's easy to understand why using the cost management techniques in this book gives a company such a large advantage over their competition. Purchased costs almost always represent a greater opportunity area than management first thinks. In fact, only after doing a good spend analysis with a strong follow-up of cost management implementation can you know for sure how competitive your company really is. You may have some real surprises!

For example, some automotive analysts believe that on average Toyota, Honda, and Nissan purchase their parts for an equivalent car at $1,600 less than their American counterparts. My experience heading up Purchasing for Honda of America Manufacturing for ten years confirms that this $1,600-per-car advantage is true. And then working for many years in Senior Management for two major auto suppliers, where I could see the full picture from a supplier's side, double confirms this fact. Your company can attain the same kind of competitive purchased cost advantage as well. Who would not enjoy such a cost advantage over their competitors?

Following the concepts of cost management, Jimmy Anklesaria describes what will help any company gain and sustain a significant cost advantage similar to that of Toyota, Honda, and Nissan. Companies such as John Deere and others have already put such practices in place. These concepts—they are not just theory—are being used every day by enlightened companies to help them compete. My guess is that your company wants to experience this strategic competitiveness as well.

Dave Nelson
Former head of Supply Management at Honda, Delphi, TRW, and John Deere; Coauthor of *Powered by Honda*, *The Purchasing Machine*, and *The Incredible Payback;* Chair Emeritus, Institute for Supply Management; Member of the Shingo Prize Academy and Board of Trustees Shingo Prize; Recipient of the J. Shipman Award, Institute of Supply Management, 2006

Acknowledgments

In September 1983, when I first came to the United States from India, had anyone told me that I would be writing books and going around the world teaching courses in Supply Chain Management, I would have fallen off my chair laughing. I was a Chartered Accountant, the British equivalent of a Certified Public Accountant, with a law degree who had come to the United States to do an MBA at the University of San Diego. I hoped to learn more about international business, finance, and marketing and then go back to rejoin the family business. All that changed when I met Professor David Burt in a marketing class in 1984. Dr. Burt had just released a book called *Proactive Procurement* and he described to me, the eternal bean counter, how senior management just did not get it when it came to the value added by the Procurement organization. His passion for the subject and genuine belief in the opportunity ahead was evident. It struck me that a person with a background in business, a professional in the field of management and cost accounting, with a law degree to boot, could bring a different perspective to the profession of procurement and supply chain management. I began to learn more about the procurement profession and shared my ideas with Dr. Burt and Warren Norquist, then Vice President of Procurement at Polaroid, about how cost accounting and financial concepts could help buyers negotiate better. They invited me to join them in coauthoring a book, *Zero Base Pric-*

ing^{TM}: *Achieving World Class Competitiveness through Reduced All-in-Cost*, published by Probus Publishing in 1990.

Even before the book was released, I traveled around the world teaching the concept to companies like Lockheed, Harris, Herman Miller, Shell Oil, Tektronix, Apple Computers, and others. Feedback from those who attended the classes was very positive and the participants in my seminars felt that they could now negotiate with more knowledge of costs than they had before taking the course. By the early 1990s the concept had been embraced by Hewlett Packard, Kodak, Deere, DuPont, Electrolux, and many other companies. More and more buyers were using *Zero Base Pricing* to negotiate better prices for goods and services and being recognized for their contribution to the bottom line of their respective companies.

Yet, something was missing. After doing a great job understanding the cost structure of a supplier and using price and cost analysis to negotiate a fair and reasonable price, buyers seemed to be hitting a brick wall. In the fall of 1991, I was having breakfast with the head of Hewlett Packard Global Procurement, Gene Richter, and he encouraged me to think about how Procurement and Engineering could collaborate with suppliers to find ways to take costs out of the supply chain. This struck a nerve with me since I had written about the importance of the Purchasing-Engineering interface in an article with Dr. Burt that was published in the *Journal of Purchasing and Materials Management* almost five years earlier. To have someone from industry back me up was most encouraging. That's when I decided to come up with a process and write another book. I tried to keep it as simple as possible so that it would be embraced by all links in the supply chain. There were a few iterations before the AIM & DRIVE process took shape and I piloted it at HP, John Deere, and Kodak. The response from buyers, engineers, other stakeholders of the customer companies, and even the suppliers, was most flattering. Yes, a true supply chain effort was taking place and collaboration was replacing confrontation with fantastic results. It was in February 1993 that I started writing a book to document the eight steps of AIM & DRIVE.

Well, here we are in 2007. Whatever happened to cycle time management? AIM & DRIVE gathered momentum as more and more companies joined the initial few and used the process to drive costs out of their supply chain. I was so busy flying around the world, raising a family, and teaching eager graduate students at the University of San Diego, that there was no time to put pen to paper. Time rolled by, the process was used by companies in the United States, Europe, Asia, Latin America, Australia, and South Africa. I was reminded by my wife, Jennifer, that the book was still not out. So, in 1997 I made another attempt at writing but gave up. No one was willing to give me more than twenty-four hours in a day and that was what I needed in order to do all the other things in my life.

It took a sad series of events to get me going again. In 2003, I lost two very influential people in my life. First to go in May was my Papa Kali. He had raised me to use common sense to solve complex problems and to explain things in language that was easy to understand. He did not get to see the book published. Then, in July that year, my mentor and friend, Gene Richter, one of the true legends in the universe of Supply Chain Management, left us behind in this world. At Gene's memorial service in Michigan, I met Patricia Moody. Tricia was writing a book with Gene, Dave Nelson (then Vice President of Supply Chain at Delphi), and Theresa Metty (at that time head of Supply Chain at Motorola). I spoke to her about my desire to complete my book as a tribute to Gene Richter and she offered to help. After three years of gentle nagging, I finally buckled down and got the book out. It is my honor to have AMACOM as my publisher and you, dear reader, as my critic. I have tried to speak from the heart, to share my experiences and those of many others who used my process across the world. There is no need for a process to be sophisticated and complex in order to be successful. I've tried to break the mold of cost accounting by looking at measuring cost in a totally different way through Formula Based Costing. Using basic algebraic formulas, users around the world have been able to establish a causal relationship between costs and cost drivers. AIM & DRIVE has proved that anyone can use the process in virtually any industry and for almost any type of cost management effort. You could use it in a multibillion-dollar company or in a small mom-and-pop business. Common sense does not have a monetary limit.

Many people have helped me in spreading the message of AIM & DRIVE around the world and getting this book out to you. My best friend ever, and wife of eighteen years, Jennifer, has been my inspiration, pillar of support, editor, and critic without whose help I would not have even attempted this undertaking. My children, Zubin, Jasmine, and Avi, have been so patient and understanding. I hope I can make up the time away from them as I traveled the world doing workshops and then dug in for a few months to finish this book.

Dr. David Burt, my friend and coauthor of *Zero Base Pricing*, is due many thanks for showing me the light and opportunity to make a difference in a totally different field from the one I had been trained.

Dr. Robert Sullivan, Dean, and JoAnne Starr, Associate Dean, of the Rady School of Management, University of California, San Diego, allowed me to share my passion and experiences with the graduate students in the new FlexMBA program. We now have future CEOs, top health care professionals, engineers, biotech scientists, founders of start-up companies, and a host of others who are energized by the supply chain processes and will be its ambassadors in the future. We will not be singing to the choir any more.

My team at the Anklesaria Group has been an immense help in implementing AIM & DRIVE at various companies around the world, bringing the theory to life. In particular, Sanjit Menezes was my sounding board when the process was in its infancy. He helped me refine the concept, provided valuable feedback, and wrote case studies that are used in my workshops. Oliver Rossi helped develop many of the worksheets in the book and was instrumental in creating an e-learning course based on this process. Dennis Kwok worked endless hours to help put the charts, figures, and worksheets together for the book.

And you, dear reader, deserve a special thanks and my gratitude for picking up this book to read. I hope that you benefit from the message, the process, worksheets, and checklists. Collaboration can succeed if there is a common, easy-to-understand, and fair process. You are the one to prove it, and I wish you the very best in your endeavor.

SUPPLY CHAIN
COST MANAGEMENT

## CHAPTER 1

Introduction

I t was a warm summer afternoon in August of 1994. I returned home to Del Mar, California, weary from the long flight from Tokyo. As I expected, there were a bunch of messages on my answering machine. One, in particular, caught my attention. It was from my mentor and good friend, Gene Richter (1937–2003), then head of Corporate Procurement at Hewlett-Packard. In his typical nonchalant voice, his message went something like this: "Jimmy, this is Gene. I wanted to let you know before you read the *Wall Street Journal* tomorrow—I've accepted a job at IBM. The challenge was too good to turn down. Anyway, we can talk about it when you get back. I'm counting on your help like you've given me at HP."

I had known Gene since 1989 when he took on the leadership of Corporate Procurement at Hewlett-Packard. He was a role model to me. It was an honor to "coach" someone like him on cost management strategies. He was such a humble person—not only willing to listen to someone twenty years his junior, but sometimes even jotting down my ideas on his ever-present three-by-five cards.

Gene joined IBM as part of Lou Gerstner's turnaround team. IBM had suffered staggering losses and there was talk of breaking up the company. Thankfully, Gerstner saw the value of one IBM, providing "solutions for a smaller planet." He recognized that the basic business equation was still the same: REVENUE − COST = PROFIT.

Mr. Gerstner asked his Chief Financial Officer to get him the "best procurement leader in the world." Gene had just led Hewlett-Packard to the *Purchasing Magazine*'s Medal of Professional Excellence. He had done this first at Black & Decker in 1988, and then again with IBM in 2000, making him the only person to lead three different companies to win this prestigious award.

When I asked Gene what his goals were, it was not surprising that he said, "The only way we can stay in business and be competitive and profitable is by following these five steps:

1. Reduce costs.

2. Reduce costs.

3. Reduce costs.

4. Reduce costs.

5. Reduce costs."

There aren't many questions in the world of business with definite answers. But try this one: "Is your company facing increasing pressure to reduce costs?" The answer is probably a resounding "Yes! You bet!"

It makes no difference whether you work for a Motorola or Nokia, Hewlett-Packard or IBM, Chevron or BP, Ford or Honda. The response is identical—cost reduction is imperative to long-term survival. It really doesn't matter whom you ask: engineers or buyers, production or sales people. Even top executives fall in the same boat. Everyone is out to reduce costs. Go ahead and ask these people the next question, "How many of you truly understand your costs?" You would think you had hit the pause and mute button on your TV set. No movement or sound. Repeat the question and ask this time for a show of hands: "How many of you can honestly say that you understand and know the costs associated with what you do in your organization?" Paralysis strikes again. Don't expect to be part of a "wave" in a football stadium. Not more than 10 percent will raise their hands. Believe me. Over the past fifteen years I've polled a few thousand executives, supply chain professionals, suppliers, and engineers in all types of companies around the world and the results are the same. Over 90 percent of people feel the pressure to manage costs and yet, fewer than 10 percent of them can honestly say that they understand the costs associated with products, services, or equipment that they are either buying or selling. It seems that managers in most companies are sending their troops out to conquer an unknown enemy. And with toy guns, too. Is it possible to reduce and manage something that most players (employees) don't even understand?

Sadly, most companies embark on a journey of managing costs only when they suffer a major loss of profits or market share. How many times have we heard CEOs make public announcements that the company will aggressively pursue a goal of cost reduction in order to be globally competitive? Then the scramble begins. Managers hurriedly schedule meetings and bark out orders. Subordinates look at one another in amazement. How can someone in a responsible position give such a stupid order? Then, they go off and do nothing, or find ways to modify the orders, or think up excuses and exceptions. Phrases like "you've got to appreciate the hidden value of what we are doing and not focus on the monetary value" are typical.

The problem isn't that costs can't be managed. It's that costs are extremely difficult to accurately define. Often, it is a question of conflicting definitions to the term "costs" that cause confusion and illogical actions. Alas, most executives fail to differentiate between cost *management* and cost *cutting*. Slashing personnel, travel, and training or R&D budgets is certainly not the way to be more competitive in the long run. It may work for state and federal governments, but not for globally competitive firms. Sure, it helps in the short run but ask yourself, "Is this sustainable?" Just look at GM and Scott Paper. They slashed costs mercilessly and what has become of them? GM is teetering on the brink of bankruptcy and Scott Paper does not even exist anymore—it's now part of Kimberly Clark.

What we need is a well-thought-out, understandable, and implementable strategy to reduce costs. The purpose of this book is to provide you and your company with a winning methodology to manage and reduce costs through the supply chain. It won't be easy. There will have to be major sacrifices and compromises, shifts in paradigms, and changes in policy. No one likes change—but change you must if you want to stay competitive. The good news is that proactive companies like IBM, HP, Motorola, Nokia, T-Mobile, Texas Instruments, Philips, Chevron, BP, Anglo American, Mercury Marine, Capital One, Nordstrom, and a few others have already embarked on the journey of Cost Management. For these companies, taking the first step was half the battle.

If we don't change our direction, we're likely to end up where we're headed. Think about where your company is heading. Do you have a clear road map on how to sustain revenue growth and implement genuine cost reduction strategies? Or are you one of those executives who feel that your job is to produce the "wow factor" with short-term results and get the heck out of the company before all hell breaks loose? This book should ignite the engine, but you are the driver and must follow the right path to a sustainable competitive advantage. Now, let's take this journey together.

## CHAPTER 2

The AIM & DRIVE Process of Cost Management

S uccessful cost management initiatives often start with a kickoff meeting to make sure everyone is on the same page. When I began working with IBM, the kickoff meeting was actually the first time that procurement managers and leaders from around the world came together.

Even though the agenda was packed, I was given a half hour to speak. I began by telling the audience that I was not there as a professor, consultant, or procurement guru, just a concerned stockholder. The previous week I had bought a fairly large number of shares of IBM at an average price of $70 (that would be $17.50 after all splits in 2007). I put up a slide that Gene Richter had used earlier in the day (see Figure 2-1) to illustrate the link between leadership, structure, and strategy. I added the part in the center.

Regardless of which part of the organization you happen to work with, the common goal of a business is to maximize stockholder wealth. At least, that's what they taught me in Finance 101. Stockholder wealth is measured by the appreciation in stock price over a period of time. And what drives the stock price? There are a bunch of financial models to calculate stock price but in layman's terms, it is the firm's earnings per share (EPS) multiplied by the price/earnings (P/E) ratio. As you can see from the top line in the center triangle of Figure 2-1, the first part of the effort to increase the stock price is to increase net profit. That means a firm has to either increase revenue with stable or lower costs, or lower costs with stable or increasing revenue. Now, what they do not tell you in business school is that the "market" does not look kindly at companies that cannot demonstrate that the revenue increase or cost reduction is sustainable. Since I was talking with Procurement folks at IBM, I stressed that point. How can we, at IBM Procurement, help the company bring top products and exceptional service to our customers? And sustain it over time? If we could work with our suppliers to take advantage of their knowledge and experience, we could increase IBM's net profit margin. That

Figure 2-1. Improving the bottom line.

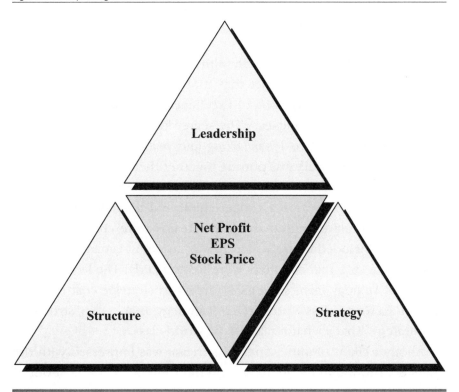

would increase the earnings per share (especially since IBM was buy-ing back a lot of shares at that time). If the P/E ratio remained the same, IBM's stock price would go up purely on the basis of an in-crease in the EPS. But, if we were to show the market that we had a strategy that is sustainable, the market would reward IBM with an even higher P/E ratio and that would magnify the impact on the stock price. All this was possible—but IBM Procurement would have to change culture, rise to the occasion, and implement some long-term strategies. I ended with a challenge to the Global Procurement team. "When I return to this same meeting in May 1997, I would like to see the stock price at $160," I said. In May 1997 my first slide read

"Thanks for taking on and meeting the $160 stock price challenge" and was signed, "a grateful stockholder." The stock had closed above $170 the previous day.

OK, so I may have gotten lucky with the stock price prediction but no one can take away the fact that IBM won the 2000 *Purchasing Magazine*'s Medal of Professional Excellence and is still a benchmark for best procurement practices. The secret formula is not that much of a secret. What IBM had was strong and visionary leadership. The next part of the formula was putting together the right structure. In a matter of months Richter had set up a dozen Commodity Councils (Category Teams) for direct procurement and a similar number of teams for indirect procurement. These teams were cross functional and global. Included in the structure was an ombudsman, whose job was to make sure that suppliers were treated fairly. The last part was an overall strategy from strategic sourcing to strategic cost management and a world-class e-procurement strategy. Leadership, structure, and strategy. That's what it takes to be world-class.

Another client of mine, Anglo American, was impressed with the IBM story but wanted more details on the strategy to take cost out of the supply chain. Anglo American was faced with low prices for many of its commodities and a weakening South African rand. Cost was very high on its agenda and an executive vice president had been brought in to execute world-class sourcing and cost management strategies. When he asked me what I would recommend, I drew him the diagram in Figure 2-2.

I explained that every CEO/COO wants the Chief Procurement Officer to deliver savings of hundreds of millions of dollars within a two- to three-year period. The problem is that they do not demand to hear how that target will be achieved or whether it is something that is sustainable.

Well, here are some basic steps that could help realize those savings. Most companies are pretty good on the negotiation side of cost

Figure 2-2. The journey from leveraging volume to leveraging ideas.

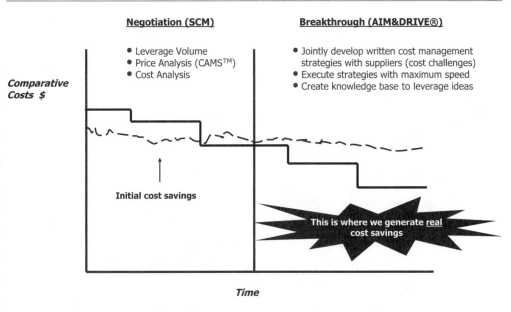

management. Unfortunately, although that brings them a good way down the path, it is not enough. At some point, there must be a change of gears as a company moves beyond negotiation and looks to breakthrough solutions to become competitive.

Before the Breakthrough

Even before a company begins the serious work of changing their procurement process, it will no doubt have taken some or all of the following steps: leveraging volume, analyzing price, and analyzing costs.

Leveraging Volume

Now, don't fall off your chair when I say that many companies have spent millions of dollars on boutique consultants who spend hundreds or thousands of hours studying the procurement process of the client only to come up with a brilliant idea: "You need to reduce your supply base and give more business to fewer suppliers." It's called trading volume for price and is clearly one of the oldest negotiation tools. Seriously, do you need a consultant to tell you the obvious? However, if you have not already done so, then it makes sense to consider how you can best leverage your spend to take advantage of volume discounts.

Analyzing Price

In some cases purchase price is the only differentiator between competing suppliers. In such cases there is no need for detailed cost analysis. *E-auctions* are becoming increasingly popular with many companies. However, there are other techniques that need to be used, such as Competitive Advantage Measurement Systems (CAMS™), which measures a firm's prices against a market index. Take the case of two category managers, one for travel and the other for metal castings. Suppose the target price reduction was 6 percent. The travel manager shows a cost increase of 3 percent while the metal castings category leader shows a savings of 9 percent. What do you think would happen in most companies? The travel manager would probably be fired while the metal castings manager would be promoted or given a nice bonus. Now, what if I told you that during the same period, metal casting prices went down 15 percent while travel prices went up 8 percent? The metal castings manager just gave up 6 percent of competitive advantage while the travel manager helped the firm achieve an advantage against the industry of 5 percent. That's why it's so important for companies to monitor prices paid for all major categories against carefully chosen market indices. Every three years you may need to do an "absolute competitiveness" study where you can benchmark your prices and processes against a carefully selected group of similar size companies in your industry as well as other industries.

Analyzing Costs

As we saw earlier, you cannot manage what you do not understand. Cost analysis is necessary to understand the cost structure in the supplier's price in order to determine whether the price is fair and reasonable. There are several kinds of cost models:

1. *Should Cost* models, which range from industry cost profiles to detailed process cost models.
2. *Price Discipline*™ models, which are used to determine a supplier's request for a price change.
3. *Total Cost of Ownership (TCO)* models, which represent the present value of all costs incurred during the life of a product, service, or equipment.

All these methods of negotiation can help a company get closer to the cost savings target set by their respective managements. The question is what to do after that. If your Chief Procurement Officer achieves the long-term target with one or more of the previously listed negotiation strategies, it simply means that the target wasn't high enough. Hence, one must plan for the next stage of cost management: breakthrough solutions.

Over the years I've seen many companies try to go beyond negotiations in their quest for greater savings. Mostly, these involve brainstorming sessions with cross-functional teams, with or without suppliers. In some cases, they deliver results while in others they are exercises in futility. The reason for this is that there does not appear to be an organized, systematic, and user-friendly process. Now, with the AIM & DRIVE process, you too should be able to reap the rewards of breakthrough savings.

Before we get into the process, it is necessary to ponder on how we got into this mess in the first place. History tends to repeat itself, so a walk down memory lane should serve us well.

Historical Perspective

1950s: The Golden Age of American Manufacturing

After World War II, apart from the United States, the rest of the world spent more than a decade rebuilding infrastructure. While the United States prided itself in being the foremost industrialized nation, Japan, West Germany, France, Great Britain, and other countries in Europe and Asia were investing in new machinery and technology. Most of their purchases were from the United States. The strong, affluent U.S. market gobbled up whatever little these countries produced for export. The 1950s were indeed the Golden Age of American heavy industry—from equipment to planes, trains, and automobiles.

1960s: The Rest of the World Catches Up

In the 1960s, while America was "high" on Elvis, the Beatles, Woodstock, and marijuana, Europe and Asia continued their march toward World Class Manufacturing. Still, the United States reigned supreme. The rest of the world was merely catching up "with our monetary help and technology," thought most American industrialists. No one cared to observe that while the average American firm used machines that were decades old, mostly reconditioned, Japan and Germany were making giant leaps in manufacturing. Using newer equipment with a dedicated and highly motivated workforce, productivity improved along with quality. The roots of "Global Competition" were beginning to take hold in the yet thin soil of these vanquished World War II countries.

1970s: The Dreadful Curse of Competition

Then came the turbulent 1970s. Apart from the Oil Crisis of 1973 and double-digit inflation, American consumers were bombarded with low-cost, high-quality goods. From automobiles to ships, hi-fi equipment to heavy machines, watches to electronics—the choices were unbelievable. To top it all, these products were not even built in the United States. Imagine that! Yes, the world had become one big market and the consumers loved it.

Not everyone thought life couldn't get any better. In boardrooms across the country, American executives were licking their wounded pride and looking for solutions. After much blaming, benchmarking, and brainstorming, a potential answer to their problems was pulled out of the hat . . . *quality!*

1980s: Can Quality Be the Answer?

And so America marched into the 1980s with renewed confidence in its ability to lead the industrialized world from the front. Companies that earlier shunned the gurus of Quality, atoned for their sins and unabashedly began to woo the great stalwarts like the late Dr. W. Edwards Deming, Joseph Juran, Dorian Shainin, and Philip Cosby. The quest for Total Quality Management (TQM) had begun. Everyone from the CEO to the line worker spent hours attending courses on TQM, Design of Experiment (DOE—a true winner), Statistical Process Control (SPC—the tail that wags the dog), Just-In-Time (JIT), Quality Functional Deployment (QFD), and Concurrent Engineering (CE). With the frenzy to educate its workforce, it's amazing that any company had time to *implement* quality.

The Malcolm Baldrige Quality Award was initiated to emphasize the need to achieve and spread the gospel of Quality. Companies like Motorola, Xerox, Cadillac, Solectron, Zytec, and others drove the message of total quality, not just through their respective firms but also through their much-reduced supplier base. Today any company that claims to be competitive will agree that most, if not all, suppliers are firm believers and practitioners of Total Quality. The non-performers have fallen by the wayside rather unceremoniously.

The critics of American quality would do well to look at Motorola's Six Sigma, Xerox's Leadership Through Quality, Tennant's Zero Defect Program, or the strides made in the area of product quality by Hewlett-Packard, Harley-Davidson, Herman Miller, and Texas Instruments, to name a few. While there is a long way to go, quality can no longer be used as a scapegoat if a firm is not competitive today.

1990s: We Can Reengineer Anything

Then came the 1990s, which could best be described as the decade of reengineering and slashing. For the first time there appeared to be a sensible approach to managing costs through the supply chain. There were gurus like Michael Hammer, who preached that processes had to be reengineered and simplified if firms were to be more competitive. Companies like IBM, Texas Instruments, Hewlett-Packard, Kodak, DuPont, Deere, Honda, and Philips, for example, discovered that working with their key suppliers led to process improvement and breakthrough cost solutions. Then again, there were the likes of GM and Scott Paper who reversed the gains of active supplier involvement in managing costs, with their short-term focus on slashing costs. The very suppliers who provided leading edge technology and quality were mercilessly dragged through the dirt in order to squeeze a couple of percentage points off their prices. The macho price slashers called this "brinkmanship." In hindsight, some would call it "stupidity." As we closed out the century the focus was on e-procurement. Or just "e" something, although most firms didn't know what they really wanted, but "e" sounded "cool."

The Twenty-First Century: The Power of the Internet Emerges

At the turn of the century, emerging nations like China and India began to pose a competitive threat to the United States, Europe, and Japan by providing the world with a highly educated workforce at a third the cost. With the Internet proving to be the great equalizer, India grew from being a cheap place for data entry to a haven for business process outsourcing (BPO), design centers, biological research, software engineering solutions, and even medical evaluation. The list will continue to grow as trade barriers come down not just in India and China but in Brazil, Russia, Bulgaria, and other eastern and central European nations.

So, here we are in the twenty-first century. What will differentiate your firm from its competition? Will it be technology? Or maybe it'll be quality and reliability? Perhaps speed of delivery? Or excellent customer service? Or do you think your firm is the only one in the industry doing e-business? The answer, dear reader, is that nowadays, frequent technological breakthroughs, high quality, reliability, on-time delivery, top customer service, and e-business are merely the *prerequisites* for being in the global race for market share. Today's customer expects this from a supplier; rather, demands it. And there are enough firms around the world that have overcome the "preliminary rounds" of technology, quality, reliability, delivery, service, and e-business.

So why should they choose your firm?

If you went shopping for a mobile phone, your choice would be, among others, a handset from Motorola, Nokia, Samsung, Lucky Goldstar, Sony-Ericson, or Sanyo. All world-class companies. All vying for your money. Which one will it be? In a few years the only differentiation will be *cost*. Companies that best manage their costs through the entire supply chain to bring you the latest technology, best quality with on-time delivery at a price lower than the others will take home the prize—your check. There's no prize for coming in second.

What Is Cost Management?

Now that you have a historical perspective, perhaps you need to seriously consider how you will drive breakthrough solutions. As I said earlier, the logical next step is to come up with a process that helps you to manage costs through the supply chain. There's no reason why this has to be complex. Cost management is a straightforward, implementable, eight-step process of AIM & DRIVE:

The Eight-Step Process: An Overview

Let's take a brief look at the overall AIM & DRIVE process, step by step (Figure 2-3).

Step 1. Agreeing on the Need to Manage Costs through the Supply Chain

Let's not waste precious time developing a strategy if it's only going to gather dust on a bookshelf. Before going further you've got to ask yourself: "Am I interested in managing costs through the supply chain, thereby becoming more competitive, along with my suppliers and customers"? If the answer is "yes" you are ready to proceed with the rest of the steps. The first step involves selecting your project, putting together a cross-functional team that includes your key supplier/s as well as internal and external stakeholders, and determining the goals of the team from different perspectives. You've got to start identifying like-minded companies in the supply chain as soon as possible. And you've got to start leading the supply chain in the AIM & DRIVE process right away. At least before other competing supply chains get their act together.

Step 2. Identifying Critical Costs in the Supply Chain

A cost that is not understood is a cost that is hard to manage. The second step involves understanding the supply chain cash flow. Money enters the supply chain only once and it's the job of the cost management team to determine how cash flows through your com-

Figure 2-3. The AIM & DRIVE process.

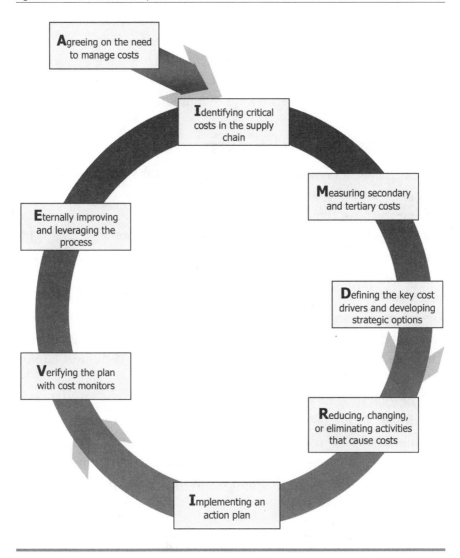

pany and your supply base. While many companies prefer not to discuss cost breakdowns with their customers, this step is a true test of a collaborative relationship. No one expects a full disclosure or "open kimono." However, unless one understands where costs are incurred in a supply chain, it becomes increasingly difficult to determine which costs are critical and therefore require more detailed analysis.

Step 3. Measuring Secondary and Tertiary Costs

Once costs are identified through the supply chain, the next stage is to apply a measurement process to each major cost or subcost. This is by far the most difficult part of cost management, yet a very critical one. Remember, a cost that is not measured is not managed. The question is: what is the best method to measure costs? Since traditional and, to some extent, even modern cost accounting systems have failed to help the users of those systems to "manage costs," we'll use a commonsense approach called Formula Based Costing that I invented only because I was so frustrated with the existing cost accounting systems. This will be explained in greater detail in Chapter 5.

The objective of Formula Based Costing is to generate a list of cost drivers through the use of algebraic equations. A cost driver is a measure of an activity that causes a cost. A driver represents a "causal relationship" between an activity and a certain cost. This means that a change in a given activity should result in a change in the cost that is driven by that activity.

Step 4. Defining Key Cost Drivers and Developing Strategic Options

The most difficult part of measuring costs is to extract a list of cost drivers. Once this is accomplished in Step 3 of the process, the next step is to select one or more drivers as key cost drivers. Selecting a driver as a key cost driver can be done by a cross-functional team, either by observation or by using a matrix described in greater detail in Chapter 6. Attention is then focused on developing a list of strategic options for the selected drivers. Strategic options tell us what makes the value of a cost driver change. This is, in effect, your databank of ideas.

Step 5. Reducing, Changing, or Eliminating Activities That Cause Costs

Costs do not disappear with the wave of a magical wand. Having defined the key cost drivers in Step 4, you need to take the list of strategic options and create strategy statements. Each strategy statement is then put through a rigorous risk-benefit analysis from different perspectives in order to identify potential strategies. Strategies are plans that are *practical* and *implementable*. They do not have to be complex or sophisticated in order to be effective. A useful strategy would be to reduce, change, or eliminate one or more of the drivers. The discussion should center on the implications of a change in a given activity. If costs are to go down, certain activities have to be eliminated or reduced. Otherwise, these costs will merely be moved to another account head or redistributed by the creative accountants of the world.

Step 6. Implementing an Action Plan

Developing an implementation plan is as critical to the cost management process as identifying a strategy and writing a strategy statement. While strategies are ideas, implementation plans are a means of converting those ideas into action. This stage involves listing the actions required for each strategy statement. The action plan consists of determining who will do what, how, and by when. Yes, even executives in industry need to be "organized" in order to successfully achieve the benefits of cost management. Why? Because it's so easy to abandon a project at this stage and go on to fight other fires.

Implementation plans, obviously, aim at successfully implementing a given strategy. It is the height of optimism to expect that all strategies will be implemented without a hitch. Murphy's Law (what can go wrong will go wrong) tends to apply from time to time and put a spoke in your wheel. It makes sense, therefore, to add another dimension to your implementation plan. This requires the creation of contingency plans: alternative strategies you will implement if your goals cannot be achieved by the proposed strategy.

Step 7. Verifying the Plan with Cost Monitors

All too often, good strategies do not realize their true potential. You may wonder why not. Perhaps a better idea came along. Not likely. In my experience, plans that fail do so because no one bothered to verify and monitor the process. The purpose of verifying the plan with cost monitors is to make sure that actions are not measured based on mere completion of an item on an action list, but by *measuring* the impact of change on the value of a given cost driver.

Step 8. Eternally Improving and Leveraging the Process

Cost management is a journey, not a destination. And the journey, like that of Total Quality Management, never ends. If the process of cost management, spelled out in the seven preceding steps, works successfully on a set of critical costs or subcosts, then it's time to start again on other costs, cost drivers, or strategic options. There's no time to stop and smell the roses. Remember that there's no patent on improvement. If you are successful, your competitors will be on your heels, putting the same strategies into practice. So, there's no time to lose; keep the wheels of cost management moving faster than those of your competitors.

Preparing for an AIM & DRIVE Exercise

It is vitally important that adequate preparation be made before conducting an AIM & DRIVE Cost Challenge. I call it a Cost Challenge because the process is designed to go beyond negotiations in order to take cost out of the supply chain. Too many times teams have gone through the process, appreciated its value and the methodology but regretted that they chose the wrong project, brought the wrong supplier, failed to get the right stakeholders from their own company, or did not come prepared with the right information. In order to make sure that this does not happen to you and your team you need to:

1. *Obtain buy-in from top management.* Top management commitment and support to the AIM & DRIVE process is critical for the success of the initiative. In Chapter 10 we will address the level of participation that is required from various executives. Not only must there be a strong message from the company's leadership but personal presence as well. It is all about "walking the talk." Employees and suppliers are burned out with the number of "fads of the month" that they are expected to follow. A Supply Chain leader who expects to play a central role in executing the AIM & DRIVE process should make it a point to have a meeting with the CEO, CFO, and other executives, show them the advantages of a collaborative way to take cost out of their product or service, and indicate to them the level of support required to make this a success. He or she should also do the public relations round with the heads of Research and Development, Marketing, Operations, Engineering, and other key functional departments. After all, the success of AIM & DRIVE is driven in large part by who attends the strategy-building session and you want to make sure that there is cross-functional representation on the team.

2. *Select key categories and top suppliers for each category.* The question that seems to crop up time and again is, which categories

are best suited for an AIM & DRIVE exercise? There is not a single category that I have seen that cannot use the process in some form or the other. Just when I think I've seen it all, something comes up that pleasantly surprises me. For example, once at Deere and Company I got a team of health practitioners working with Deere to reduce the cost of health care in general and cardiac cases in particular. What a wonderful session that was. Having doctors, surgeons, and administrators giving us ideas on how to reduce the rate of incidents and the importance of preventive medicine was a lesson for all of us analytical folks. Companies that have successfully implemented AIM & DRIVE have done so because they first determined which categories to start with; they put a few successes under their belts and then rolled out the other categories. For each major category or subcategory it becomes necessary to choose the right supplier to attend the strategy-building session. Supplier selection can be made based on the volume of business with particular suppliers or on the level of the relationship. Some large suppliers are reluctant to share cost information or cost savings ideas with most customers. A smaller supplier, on the other hand, may be hungry for the business and willing to do what it takes to get it. In many cases I have noticed that smaller companies tend to send people to the AIM & DRIVE session that are decision makers and very knowledgeable about the operations of the company. Many times it is the owner or founder who is part of the team. Larger companies will tend to load their team with global account managers, regional account managers, customer relationship managers, and sales folks who, with due respect, may not be ideal for coming up with breakthrough solutions. If the objective is to *harness the inherent knowledge of the extended enterprise,* it makes sense to invite more than one supplier for each major category or subcategory. Some companies may select two key suppliers per category; while I have seen others select as many as a dozen. IBM invited fourteen key suppliers for air, ocean, and ground transportation to attend an AIM &

DRIVE workshop in Guadalajara, Mexico. At first, I was a bit taken aback to see competitors in the same room. But they understood that, as preferred suppliers to IBM, they had to work together to help IBM streamline its logistics processes—and AIM & DRIVE was the process we would use to make this happen. The response was phenomenal and I have yet to see so many companies providing such a wonderful list of valuable ideas in front of their competitors. They all realized that they were working for the same customer. So, selecting the right supplier and having them send the right people are a must if you are to successfully implement an AIM & DRIVE strategy. And, yes, those right people must have the right attitude too.

3. *Brief customer/supplier team leaders.* Having selected the categories and suppliers for an AIM & DRIVE exercise, it is necessary to brief the leaders of each of these categories and supplier representative. Gene Richter always made sure that the leadership of IBM's key suppliers was invited to a half-day meeting along with the leaders of the Commodity Councils that were required to build their respective cost management strategies. He would address the meeting with a clear signal to all invited suppliers that IBM was looking to them for help in providing the best solution to its customers. Cost was mentioned as an important differentiator along with technology, quality, delivery, service levels, and so on. I would then give them a quick overview of the process, expectations, and time lines. We ran a case study so that both IBM-ers and suppliers got a hands-on experience of the process and could relate to it when they determined which topic to choose and who to bring along to the AIM & DRIVE session. Today, few companies are willing to fund such meetings so we resort to teleconferences where suppliers and team leaders are briefed about the expectations and given an overview of AIM & DRIVE.

4. *Determine resource requirements.* A company must go into the AIM & DRIVE process with its eyes open and a full understanding

of the resources required to make it happen. If you want to do it correctly you need to come up with the budget for a team to get together and have the right people present. The supplier has to agree on this as well. There is no point scheduling a face-to-face meeting between a buyer and salesperson when both companies want to save on travel costs. If that's the issue, it is better to do the whole exercise over a teleconference with the right people in attendance. As technology improves, teleconferencing is becoming more and more popular. I still maintain that there is nothing better than a face-to-face meeting, especially for the first session. However, I understand the demands on people's time and the budget constraints they face. A major electronics manufacturer asked me whether I would help roll out AIM & DRIVE across the global categories within a two-year time frame. Suppliers and category teams were spread across the globe but mainly in the United States and Asia. In the same breath I was told that the company had a freeze on travel so they could not send engineers to the meetings if it involved travel. We tried one in China without the key engineers who were in the United States. It was a disaster. Realizing the importance of having the right people present, I offered to fund the travel budget of three or four key people, provided the team would be given 2 percent of the savings from their strategy to fund the rest of the program (and reimburse me, of course). They took me up on my offer and in the very first Cost Challenge with a supplier of batteries, the team realized savings of $9.7 million within four months. The Vice President of Supply Chain managed to convince the CFO that 2 percent of that amount should be reinvested in the team and the rest of the program. This fueled the engine and in less than two years the company had documented savings of over a billion dollars. No one ever questioned the budget for travel for AIM & DRIVE programs again. Again, it takes the commitment of monetary and human resources to successfully implement AIM & DRIVE. Think seriously about this commitment before you launch on the journey.

5. *Educate participants in the AIM & DRIVE process.* With executive buy-in, key categories and suppliers selected and briefed, and the resources committed, it is time to educate the team members in the AIM & DRIVE process. I've seen this done a couple of ways. One would be the approach followed by TI, IBM, Kodak, DuPont, Deere, Mercury Marine, Hewlett-Packard, Agilent, Philips, and others. These companies held two-day events where between four and eight supplier teams were invited to participate. For about two thirds of the first day I went through the AIM & DRIVE process and templates, gave a lot of examples, and had everyone do a case study to get used to the templates. Then the teams went to their respective breakout rooms to begin applying the process to their project. At the end of the second day we would bring the teams back together for a presentation to the executives and the rest of the class. Sometimes if teams felt uncomfortable sharing their strategies with competing suppliers present, we had the individual presentations in the breakout room or the competing supplier was asked to step outside during the general session.

Nordstrom, Motorola, Nokia, Chevron, Anglo American, and a few others held a one-day training session followed by a gap of a few weeks and then held one-on-one Cost Challenges with the suppliers that attended those training sessions. This obviously took more time and resources—but the level of detail was substantially higher.

With this book, there should not be a problem of educating the teams. By the time you have read the whole book you should be ready to actively participate in a Cost Challenge using the AIM & DRIVE process. The next eight chapters will take you through the process, step by step. Let's roll up our sleeves and get into the AIM & DRIVE process of collaboration to take cost out of your supply chain.

Checklist for Preparing for an AIM & DRIVE Exercise

❑ Chart out where you are on the journey from leveraging volume
to leveraging ideas.

❑ Determine whether you are ready for an AIM & DRIVE exercise.

❑ Make a buy-in presentation to top management.

❑ Select key categories and top suppliers for each.

❑ Send invitations to stakeholders and key suppliers.

❑ Brief customer/supplier team leaders on the AIM & DRIVE process.

❑ Determine resource requirements (both monetary and human).

❑ Educate participants.

❑ Schedule strategy sessions.

Agreeing on the Need
to Manage Costs

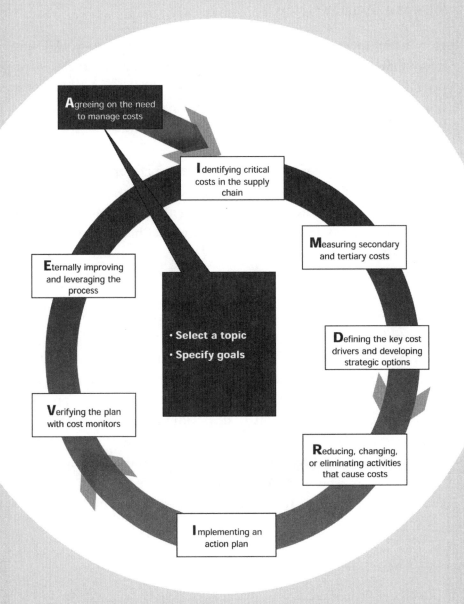

There is no point trying to manage costs if the respective links of the supply chain do not agree to the need and work together to take costs out of the chain. What is required is a concerted effort from all sides to work, make sacrifices, and eventually change the way they do business.

What Is a Strategy?

How many meetings have you attended over the past week? How many times did you hear the word "strategy" or "strategic" mentioned? A lot, I bet. You know, many times we use words in business because they sound "cool" or "in" or "managerial." Often, we really don't know the meaning and implication of the words we use as part of business jargon.

The word "strategy" can be defined as a plan or method for obtaining a specific goal or result. It is a series of ideas, actions, and methodologies that direct a team, organization, company, or supply chain toward a common, predefined goal. A Chinese General, Sun Tzu, in his excellent book on strategy, *The Art of War,* likens a strategy to a river. Like a spring it originates with a concept or idea. It follows one clear direction—a river can only flow downhill toward another larger body of water. Along the way, other ideas and players with a common focus join the team and move in the same direction—a river is joined by tributaries and other rivulets that move in the same direction as the main river. When a problem is encountered, the strategy team falls back on its preagreed plan of action to tackle the problem, using innovation and flexibility to deal with unforeseen situations—a river may encounter a rock or other obstacle and will find its way around, under, or through, even if it finally ends up creating the Grand Canyon. The goal of a strategy should be well defined and known to all parties—a river has a clear destination and that may be a large lake, sea, or ocean. Finally, a good strategy, like a river, will not turn back and disappear just because of an obstacle in its path.

In the AIM & DRIVE process, the first step for a team is to clearly set out its goals from different perspectives. While one can expect to see a goal of reducing the financial cost of a product or service, that goal alone is not enough. There are others in a team who think of costs quite differently. Marketing may want to reduce time-to-market, manufacturing may feel it important to maintain a smooth flow of production, while logistics may want to maintain the lowest possible level of inventory. Ultimately, it is the combined goal of the team that needs to be achieved, not one special interest group or function.

Do We Really Need Strategies?

Many managers are of the view that strategies are not required in managing costs. These are the majority, unfortunately, who grew up in the days of negotiation. You still cannot help but read advertisements in various in-flight magazines urging the unsuspecting reader to effectively negotiate. "You don't get what you deserve, you get what you negotiate," the ads cry out. And many a manager would say, "Amen." Well that's fine if you're negotiating to buy a used car or bargaining with a little kid trying to sell you a "genuine imitation" Rolex in the back alleys of Hong Kong. Most world-class suppliers will walk away from a bargain-hunting customer. And why not? Surely a supplier who is considered world-class has a string of companies outside its door, each begging to be one of the privileged customers.

The days of the hatchet are over. One cannot expect to slash costs by barking out orders from the top. "Cut head count, cut travel, cut training, cut R&D, cut supplier profits, cut, cut, cut . . ." There has to be a common focus in order for a supply chain to compete in this fiercely competitive marketplace. Consider what is common between various links in the chain. Cutting margins can hardly be called a common focus. I haven't seen many companies screaming "please cut my margins because I'm making so much money, it hurts." Have you? Instead, a successful supply chain looks at the lifeblood of the chain and that is the ultimate customer. It is this customer that puts money into the supply chain when he/she buys the product or service. This may sound terribly capitalistic but it is money that makes the world of business go around. Try running a business without money coming in the door. It's time we all appreciate the end customer—and do whatever it takes to get him or her to part with money time after time.

The concept of customer satisfaction is giving way to customer delightment. Delighting the customer is delivering goods or services with the leading technology, world-class quality, excellent service, on time every time, being socially and environmentally conscious, and all this at a lower cost than the competing supply chain.

The Best Have to Get Better

In my travels around the world, I've run into all sorts of companies. It's interesting to note that the ones who lead their respective markets are the ones engaging in the development of cost management strategies. IBM, Hewlett-Packard, Motorola, Nokia, Chevron, BP, Anglo American, Texas Instruments, and Deere are all leaders in their respective industries. They have used strategic initiatives, including the AIM & DRIVE process, to develop clear strategies to manage costs with their key suppliers. You would expect these companies to sit back on their laurels and count their profits. No. Doing that would mean forgetting what happened to the Greeks, Romans, the British, and perhaps even the United States. These countries became the benchmarks of their times in trade and commerce. Then they rested on their laurels and other civilizations emulated them and did things even better. By the time these countries woke up, it was too late. In business, it's the number-one company that is always benchmarked by the competition. And, why not? You don't expect a company to emulate the worst competitor in the industry, do you? Call it copying, emulating, competitive analysis, benchmarking, or the latest politically correct term. Your job should always be to see what your number-one competitor is doing. Copy it and do it better. In America we complained when the Japanese did this. We called that unfair trade. Today, we do it blatantly and call it "benchmarking." Just like when a student paraphrases from an article, he or she is accused of plagiarizing. When a professor does the same it's called "research." How hypocritical!

Demonstrating Leadership in the Supply Chain

Most companies in the supply chain are reluctant to talk about costs. One reason may be that most of them do not truly understand their costs. That's quite understandable as we saw earlier in the introduction. It takes a leader to bring the chain together. That leader must be a company that is willing to share the idea of a supply chain that joins together to write and implement cost management strategies, without getting into the hidden secrets of one another. Remember, in developing a cost management strategy you do not have to share *detailed* cost data, but you must show a willingness to share relevant information and work toward a common goal of reducing both supplier and customer costs.

I've had the honor of working with some of the best companies in the world for almost twenty years. Texas Instruments (TI) is one of my benchmarks for leadership in the supply chain cost management process. In the early 1990s, under pressure from one of its key customers, TI began to seriously work on developing a process of managing costs through the supply chain as opposed to cutting costs only when the customer screamed. Senior management took up the challenge to implement the process within two years. In August 1993 I addressed the worldwide commodity management teams on the need to manage costs. They were given an overview of the AIM & DRIVE philosophy and encouraged to abandon the hatchet. By December we had obtained buy-in from the vice chairman. In the first eight months of 1994, more than 600 TI'ers around the world were trained in the AIM & DRIVE methodology. Once we were confident that the message had reached most of those who dealt with suppliers, we shifted our focus to educating the supply base.

Starting in August 1994, top executives of about 100 supplier companies from the United States, Asia, and Europe were invited to Dallas to go through a two-day session on the AIM & DRIVE process. The objective was to share the process and communicate what TI expected from a strategic supplier and what the company was willing to do on its part. Having obtained the "buy-in" from these managers, 1995 became the "year of deployment." With the total support of top management across the divisions, we held eighteen workshops around the world. By now nearly 200 supplier representatives had been exposed to the methodology and had joined TI in writing a joint cost management strategy.

Feedback from suppliers was most encouraging. TI was slowly but surely moving toward a totally new type of relationship with its key suppliers: a relationship based on respect and admiration for one another that would result in a competitive advantage for both sides. Many skeptics said that this would not work, especially with the Japanese. We proved them wrong. More than sixty Japanese suppliers participated in the AIM & DRIVE workshops and implemented strategies that saved millions of dollars.

Some of the suppliers went a step further. Recognizing cost management as a potential differentiator, some suppliers used the AIM & DRIVE process with a few of their key customers to take costs out of the supply chain. Some of the savings flowed down to the immediate customer and sometimes all the way down to the end customer. Do

you think a customer who benefited from this would even look at another supplier on the next contract? Not likely.

TI is not the only company to demonstrate leadership through the supply chain. Gene Richter brought IBM back into reckoning with the rapid deployment of collaborative cost management strategies across production as well as non-production suppliers, saving over $5 billion in two years. IBM was one of the first companies to expand these strategies to their Marketing and Communication (Marcom) expenditure. It took time for IBM Global Procurement's Marcom Council to convince their marketing colleagues that Procurement could help them better manage their billion-plus-dollar spending. There was some skepticism about the AIM & DRIVE process. But by the end of the day marketing executives were convinced that the process would work. IBM's director of MARCOM business operations set up a series of workshops where we worked on the development and production of advertising campaigns, trade shows, and special events. What is particularly important is that in many cases, instead of cutting the budget, IBM was able to buy more advertising for the same budget as before. Both IBM and its supplier agreed that the process had helped them streamline their operations and, in fact, had even succeeded in strengthening the business relationship. There have been similar initiatives at Philips, Anglo American, Nordstrom, Mercury Marine, Eastman Kodak, DuPont, Arizona Public Service, and John Deere. This list goes on. These companies demonstrated leadership in their respective supply chains. By motivating suppliers to go beyond negotiations and work together in a collaborative way, they were able to reach some unreachable heights.

Facilitating the Right Decision-Making Process

All the companies mentioned shared the AIM & DRIVE process with key suppliers in their respective supply chains. At no time did they dictate to the supply base that "this is the process you will follow with us, or else!" Instead, they invited the top executives of key suppliers to review the AIM & DRIVE process. If a supplier had a problem using the AIM & DRIVE process for any reason, it was up to them to suggest an alternate process of managing costs. However, those suppliers that refused to do either were clearly sending a message to the customer company that they did not "agree" on the need to manage costs and did not believe in a collaborative relationship with that customer.

You may wonder, "Why do you insist on a *process* of managing costs. Aren't the results enough?" In the short run you may be right. However, a process is like a thread that binds the fabric of the supply chain together. Especially when times are bad for the industry, it is a common, well-established, and implementable process that will facilitate the right decision. Also, costs mean different things to different people within an organization and between companies. A common process for managing costs is the only way to prevent the chain's "special interest groups" from tugging in opposite directions while making decisions.

Building Credibility and Respect

Using the AIM & DRIVE process through the supply chain requires a lot of discipline. The companies that introduced this process were first looked on with a great deal of suspicion. Even when suppliers or customers agreed to work together on the process, there were times when the whip needed to be cracked in order to keep the teams on track with their respective implementation plans.

No one said that discipline was something we all like. In fact, all you have to do is remember a strict parent or a school teacher who disciplined you when you were a kid. Weren't there times when you hated them for disciplining you? Well, what do you think now? Speaking for myself, I'm glad for the discipline I received and respect those who meted it out to me. The same goes for disciplining the supply chain. Many suppliers who have been through the AIM & DRIVE process have commented that their only regret is that they were not subjected to the process earlier.

The Goal of Cost Management Strategies

Even though it appears that the focus of cost management strategies is to reduce cost, it is obvious that in the long run there will be times when costs will inevitably increase. If not, then theoretically, at some point down the road, you would expect to buy something and have your supplier deliver the product or service along with a check in your favor. As I said earlier, the first step in the AIM & DRIVE process is to agree to "manage" costs. As long as your supply chain costs are consistently lower than that of your competing supply chain, you have a *sustained competitive advantage*. It means that in good times you are able to make a higher profit than your competitor if your sales prices are the same. And if the market heads south, why then, you will lose less than your competition and live to fight another day.

Well, are you ready to go through the process now? Let's join a team at "Anything Inc." that is facing a problem of cost overruns on a "Zigmo."

The Story of Anything Inc.

Once upon a time there was a company called Anything Inc. One day Anything Inc. introduced a new product into the market, a $300 Zigmo. The unit was targeted toward the low end of the Zigmo market where prices ranged from $200 to $600. Zigmos were doing extremely well and sales were projected at

1,000,000 units per year for at least the next three years. Costs were estimated as follows:

1. Direct Material	$150
2. Direct Labor	$ 15
3. Manufacturing OH	$ 45
4. General, Selling, & Admin.	$ 75
5. Profit	$ 15
Selling Price	$300

A year went by and everything seemed to be going well. Actual sales were 1,003,112 units. A review meeting was held to evaluate the year's performance and discuss strategy for the one ahead. It was at this meeting that the first shock was felt.

It all began when Mr. Ido Makitall, the manufacturing manager, turned to Mr. Bill Dollar, the CFO, and requested additional funding for process improvements. Mr. Dollar's reply caught everyone by surprise. "I'm sorry," he said, "We have no money."

Minor pandemonium broke out. "What do you mean by no money?" screamed Ms. Mee Bie Cheep, the purchasing manager. "We came in 3.3 percent below budget in our department, something we worked very hard toward. That's $5 straight to the bottom line."

"Our conversion costs were just $2 per unit over budget, well within a reasonable limit considering the rate of inflation last year," said Mr. Makitall.

"We too came in on budget," Ms. Rhea Design, the R&D manager, added.

All eyes turned to Mr. Ican Sell, the marketing manager, who looked very sheep-ish. "We were $15 per unit over budget," he said with a tone of sadness. "Our customer service costs were $25 per unit. We budgeted only for $10 per unit." Needless to say, all present thought the same thing, what in the world had happened? As if reading their minds, Mr. Sell continued, "All our estimates were based on projected sales of 1,000,000 units. In order for us to reach those targets, our sales people were forced to give our corporate customers some very special warranty provisions."

"And what might those be?" inquired Mr. Makitall.

"We gave them a one-year warranty," Sell replied.

"Surely that couldn't have cost us $15,000,000 more," said Ms. Cheep.

"Absolutely not," returned Mr. Sell, "but we agreed to give them a forty-eight-hour turnaround. The number of calls we've received this past year was more than we had anticipated."

One could almost hear the silence. Five minutes went by. "Well," stated Mr. Dollar, breaking the awkwardness of the moment. "Let's not cry over spilt milk. What are we going to do about it?"

"How about an AIM & DRIVE session on the cost of Customer Service?" suggested Ms. Cheep. They all looked at one another. A unanimous affirmative nod said it all.

And so it was that the Zigmo team began its quest for data on the cost of customer service for goods under warranty. A summary of the various activities and costs associated with Customer Service follows:

1. Calls to Customer Service (Anything Inc.)

A twenty-four-hour customer service desk had been established for all products manufactured by Anything Inc. All calls regarding the Zigmo were directed to this Help Desk. These calls ranged from basic inquiries to complex problems with the unit. Since operators at the service desk were not technically qualified, they were only able to assist callers who had informational questions. All problems relating to the unit were transferred to the Technical Service Center at Fixit, Inc., a subcontractor. In the past twelve months, 300,000 calls were received by the Help Desk, of which 200,000 were transferred to Fixit, Inc. The average call to the Help Desk lasted two minutes. The Customer Service Department billed the Zigmo product line at the rate of $0.50 per minute, according to the newly installed activity based costing (ABC) system.

2. Calls to Fixit, Inc.'s Technical Service Center (TSC)

In keeping with the company's strategy of focusing on its core competency and outsourcing all other activities, Anything Inc. had recently spun off one of its repair centers, Fixit, Inc. Most of the technicians of Fixit, Inc. had previously worked for Anything Inc. and had been thoroughly trained on the Zigmo.

Of the 200,000 telephone calls that were received by Fixit, Inc.'s TSC in the past twelve months, 136,000 were solved by the Fixit technicians. Only 1,000 of these required parts (the rest were minor problems that the customer could handle). When required, spare parts were ordered from Fixit's Regional Service Center (RSC) and shipped to the customer either from inventory or after procuring them in the market. The old parts that were replaced were shipped (collect) to the RSC by the customer. These were then disassembled, sorted, and stored at the RSC if they were capable of being reused. If not, the parts were scrapped.

An average call to the Fixit Technical Center lasted four minutes, for which Anything Inc. was billed at the rate of $150 per hour ($2.50 per minute). For the 1,000 calls that needed parts, Fixit billed an average of $70 per order. This $70 charge included $40 for parts based on an average of two parts per job, at $20 per part. Freight for sending back the old parts and shipping the replacement ones was budgeted at $10 for each shipment of two parts weighing approximately 0.8 kg each. The shipping rate was negotiated at $6.25 per kg. Fixit was charged $10 for disposing the replaced parts.

3. Field Service

Of the 200,000 calls that were transferred to Fixit, as mentioned earlier, 136,000 were solved over the phone. The balance of 64,000 that could not be solved, either because of a complex problem or because of the type of customer involved, were transferred to a field service representative. The field service rep would visit the customer and attempt to solve the problem at the customer's location. Such service calls averaged two hours each and were billed at a fully loaded rate of $150 per hour. While it certainly did not take two hours to solve most problems, one field rep had remarked that half the time was spent getting to the customer, waiting in lobbies while security experienced their "power trips" before letting the rep into the offices or plants, and filling in tons of paperwork.

The field service technicians were able to solve 90 percent of the problems at the customers' sites. Of these, 2,800 required parts (charged out at the same $70 as before). This worked out to $196,000 per year (2,800 × $70).

4. Replacement and Repairs

For the 10 percent (6,400) of field service repairs that could not be solved by the technician, the customers were provided with a replacement unit. The charge to the warranty budget was a full sale price of $300. The old units were shipped back to the Regional Service Center at Fixit Inc. at an average freight cost of $20 per unit. In the past year, 70 percent (4,480 defective units) were repaired at an average cost of $85 each. The $85 repair charge was based on an estimate of 18 minutes of labor per repair at $150 per hour, plus $40 for parts. After repairs, the units were "fed into the pipeline" to be used for future replacements. The transfer price resulted in "revenue" of $225 per unit to the RSC. Thus the net cost for every replaced unit was $180 ($300 charge for a new unit, plus $20 to ship the old unit back, plus $85 to repair the old unit, minus $225 revenue for "selling" the repaired unit back to inventory).

5. Dismantling and Scrapping

As can be seen in the section above, 4,480 of the 6,400 returned units were repaired and fed into the pipeline. The remaining 1,920 irreparable units were dismantled, sorted, and after salvaging some parts, the rest were scrapped. This dismantling activity was charged out at $10 per unit. Therefore the cost for each of the 1,920 such units would be $330 ($300 charge for the new unit replaced, plus $20 to ship the old unit back, plus $10 to dismantle the old unit).

Bill Dollar calculated the total cost of the entire process to be around $23.2 million (see Figure 3-1). In order to bring the project cost down by $15 million something dramatic would need to be done. Will the team at Anything Inc. live happily ever after? Let's go through the rest of the story and see for ourselves.

I guess you could say that the team had no choice but to "agree" to manage the cost of customer service. Two other teams wanted to go through the same process so it was decided to add the "Printed Manuals" category team that worked on the user manuals for the Zigmo and the Packaging Category Team that chose to work on one type of corrugated box that carried spare parts to and from customers. As we go through the rest of the book we will stay with the Customer

Figure 3-1. Estimated cost of customer service for goods under warranty.

	Details of Activities	Formula (if any)	Estimated Amount
1	300,000 calls to Customer Service Center (avg. 2 minutes per call @ $0.50 per minute)	(300,000 × 2 × $0.50)	$300,000
2	200,000 calls transferred to Fixit, Inc.'s Technical Service Center (TSC) @ 4 minutes per call. Service rate: $150/hour	(200,000 ÷ 15 × $150)	$2,000,000
3	Cost of parts needed for 1,000 calls solved by TSC @ $70 each	[1,000 × $(40 + 20 + 10)]	$70,000
4	64,000 field service calls (avg. 2 hours per call @ $150/hour)	(64,000 × 2 × $150)	$19,200,000
5	Cost of parts needed for field service calls (90% of calls were solved of which 2,800 needed parts @ $70 each)	(2800 × $70)	$196,000
6	Cost of defective units shipped backed to Regional Service and repaired. 4,480 out of 6,400 repaired at a net cost of $180 each	[4,480 × $(300 + 20 + 85 − 225)]	$806,400
7	Cost of defective units shipped back to RSC that were scrapped. 1,920 units were scrapped at a net cost of $330	[1,920 × $(300 + 20 + 10)]	$633,600
	Total cost of Customer Service for goods under warranty		**$23,206,000**

Service team at Anything Inc. as a primary team. However, it helps to see the progress of the other teams in order to get a flavor of the versatility of the AIM & DRIVE process.

Preparing for a Cost Management Strategy-Building Session

Before you can get out there and organize a cost management workshop, there are a number of tasks you will need to perform.

Review Business Plan and Procurement/Marketing Strategy

Before beginning to battle costs, it makes sense to spend half an hour reviewing the business plan of the company or companies represented. You need to know the reason why you are in this business, what your corporate goals are, who the target customer is—both today and in the future—what the business environment that affects your product/service in the market is, and so on. At the same time, if you are dealing with a supplier, you need to be open and honest in sharing your procurement strategy: what kind of supply base are you looking for, current and future plans, single or multiple sources, local or global, expected volume of business, new opportunities and threats, technology road maps, and other information that can help a supplier plan for the future. A supplier, on the other hand, needs to share its marketing plan with its key customers: what does it expect from a world-class customer; what new products, services, or added value does it have to offer; what are its plans for expansion, diversification, or divestment. If nothing else, the sharing of such plans gives both parties a feeling of mutual trust and a willingness to work together toward a common goal like managing costs.

Identify Initial Participants for the Team

There is no reason to create a large cost management team until you have chosen a critical cost to manage. However, initially a group of high-level managers will have to meet and decide on the topic or topics for developing a written cost management strategy. At IBM, Gene Richter created Commodity Councils and left it to the Council leaders to determine which product or service suppliers were to be invited to start the process of writing a cost management strategy. Executives from some of the major suppliers to IBM were then invited and presented with information and future plans never before shared by "Big Blue" with its suppliers. It was amazing to see how much the suppliers were willing to share once they saw IBM opening up.

Select Primary Cost/s to Be Managed

Remember the definition of the word "strategy"? It is defined as a "plan or method for obtaining a specific goal or result." If we follow Sun Tzu's logic, managing total cost is a process of identifying and managing smaller elements of cost that make up the total. It's hard to put together one team to manage the total cost of an automobile, or a phone, or a giant construction project. Instead, there would need to be a number of smaller teams working on different categories, components, or services. The question is: how does one decide which costs need to be managed through a written strategy? There are various ways of determining this:

1. *Pareto Analysis:* choosing those costs that constitute a significant percentage of the total cost.

2. *Significant Competitive Gap:* where a certain cost line item may or may not be a large percentage of the total cost, but benchmarking exercises show that the competition is spending significantly less on that cost item.

3. *Variation from Established Standard That Causes Profitability to Be Jeopardized:* when product pricing is set based on a standard cost system and the actual cost of one or more line items indicates a significant negative variance.

4. *Spend Exceeds a "Hurdle" Amount:* where management establishes that any team that spends more than a given amount of money should have a written cost management strategy in addition to its negotiation strategy.

5. *Topic Can Be Leveraged:* when the team determines that ideas from this topic can be used across other products or by other divisions in the company.

At Anything Inc. the initial team of Makitall, Dollar, Cheep, Sell, and Design filled in the worksheet in Figure 3-2 for the Zigmo and concluded that even though the cost of customer service was not very significant compared to the sales price, the fact that it was 150 percent ($15) above the budgeted figure was enough of a reason to consider customer service a *critical cost*. Besides, with a sales volume of about one million Zigmos, the annual expenditure on customer service would be around $23.2 million. This is the cost they agreed to manage.

The purpose of the worksheet in Figure 3-2 is for the initial team to write down why they chose a specific topic as their primary cost.

Figure 3-2. Selection of primary cost and rationale for customer services for goods under warranty.

AIM & DRIVE: Agreeing to Manage Costs

Primary Cost:	Customer Service - Warranty
Total Spend:	$23,206,000
Leverageable Spend:	$150,000,000

Rationale for Choosing Primary Cost:
Customer service costs were $13,206,000 over budget
Amount spent is well over the hurdle amount
The strategies can be leveraged across other products of Anything Inc.

As you can see in this example, Customer Service was considered because those costs were $13,206,000 over budget and needed to be reduced dramatically if Anything Inc. were to be profitable. Besides, some of the ideas from this strategy could possibly be leveraged across customer service costs for other products of the company.

Put Together the Rest of the Cost Management Team

Having selected the "topic" for a written cost management strategy the initial team members will need to consider just who else needs to be included. This is a tough call. On the one hand you don't want to have an unusually large group of people. Yet, it helps to have different perspectives in your quest to write an implementable cost management strategy. There is no magic formula, unfortunately. The decision will have to be made on a case-by-case basis. Here is a start:

1. A decision maker: if suppliers are involved, then you'll need at least one decision maker for each link of the supply chain.

2. Ten-meter managers: this term is used to describe people who are closest to the action or activity that causes the cost/s you are attempting to manage.

3. Standby consultants: these are professionals from within or outside the companies participating in the strategy session who may need to be called in for clarification or expert opinion even though they may not be needed right through the session.

The team at Anything Inc. decided to include at least the following people:

1. A senior telephone operator from the Customer Service Center

2. An engineer and a supervisor from Fixit's Technical Service Center

3. The Purchasing and Logistics manager of Fixit, Inc.

4. A senior field service engineer from Fixit

5. A repair technician from Fixit

6. Fixit's financial controller

When you run your own AIM & DRIVE session please remember that the new members you coopt should be able to add value to the team with their experience and expertise in their respective fields. I've found that too often companies try to load up the team with managers. Not a good idea. You really ought to be looking at people who are closest to the activity: the ten-meter managers. After all, these are the people who see the parts or use the service or capital equipment.

Determining Team Goals

Just as it's vital that your team be composed of the right people from the right departments—with the right attitude—it's important that the team have the right goals and the right focus.

It is always tempting to focus on monetary goals in a cost management strategy session. After all, that is what management wants to see, isn't it? Real cost savings. While that is no doubt true, the fact that the team has been expanded to include subject matter experts from different functional areas, including suppliers where necessary, forces you—fortunately—to consider their perspectives as well. Think about how you would feel if you were a marketing manager and were in a meeting where the goal of increasing market share was not even considered a topic for discussion. Or, if you were a quality engineer and no one considered product quality to be of any importance. You would seriously question why you were at this meeting and would certainly not give your best efforts to the team. That's why I strongly recommend opening the discussion to include goals from different perspectives. Apart from making all participants feel included, it is critical that the focus be on the *total solution* and not just price reduction.

In many cost management strategy sessions that I have facilitated I have found that teams push themselves only as far as the expectation of their leaders. That is why it is so important to select team leaders who are able to set realistic stretch goals for their respective teams and motivate them to push themselves. I remember once working with a team from a leading mobile phone manufacturer who had invited a Japanese supplier that made motors for the handset. The cost of the motor had been reduced from around $3.50 to under $3.00. That's over 10 percent. However, the team leader challenged the team to look at a figure below $1.00. The initial reaction was one of disbelief, but the team buckled down and gave it a shot. And, what would you know? They achieved it within six months. I also remember one of the Sourcing Directors, with tongue in cheek, commenting that perhaps the team could go even further and knock the cost down below $0.50. Yes, fifty cents. Even I thought that it was going too far, but the Japanese supplier took it seriously and asked that the AIM & DRIVE effort continue another four months. I can proudly say that by the time we were done, the motor cost less than $0.50. What a tribute to the leader of the team, the incredible ideas from the supplier, and the willingness of all to take on a stretch goal like this! It only goes to show that with determination and a "never say never" attitude, the sky is the limit.

Figure 3-3 illustrates the goals that the Customer Service team of Anything Inc. put together. Notice that some of the goals are not easy to quantify while others can be quantified quite easily. For example, it is easy to measure a 5 percent profit margin or a 6 percent increase

Figure 3-3. Goals specification worksheet for customer services for goods under warranty (customer and supplier goals).

AIM & DRIVE: Agreeing to Manage Costs

Goals for Anything Inc:

Finance	Achieve a 5% profit margin
Marketing	Increase market share of Zigmos by 6%
Quality	Meet customer's product and service quality expectations
Procurement	Standardize parts for the Zigmo
Procurement	Obtain lowest Total Cost of Ownership of the customer service solution

Goals for Fixit Inc:

Finance	Achieve a 7% profit margin
Marketing	Provide Anything Inc. customers with world-class service with quick turnaround time
Logistics	Avoid shipment of parts by airfreight
Quality	Maintain high quality of repairs
Service Center	Optimize service center workload
Field Service	Maximize productive worktime

---

in market share. It would be a lot harder to measure something like "provide world-class customer service." Nevertheless, these qualitative goals are equally important and while they may be difficult to measure, you could always consider a way of putting subjective goals on a scale from 1 to 5, where 5 represents the team's opinion that the goal has been fully met and the numbers 1 through 4 represent levels of progress that have been made.

The Master Worksheet

At the end of a strategy-building session a team will find it useful to have a brief summary of their work. The Master Worksheet in Figure 3-4 is something that team spokespeople have found extremely valuable as they make a presentation to top management. We'll begin

Figure 3-4. Master worksheet for customer service.

AIM & DRIVE: Master Worksheet

A PRIMARY COST : CUSTOMER SERVICE FOR GOODS UNDER WARRANTY

Total Spend = $23,206,000

CRITICAL COSTS	COST DRIVERS	KEY COST DRIVERS	SELECTED STRATEGY STATEMENT	ACTION ITEMS		WHO	DUE DATE
I	M	D	R	I		VE	VE

filling in the Master Worksheet as we go along. For now, all you will see is the selection of the primary cost, Customer Service for Goods under Warranty. Later, you will see the Master Worksheet evolve into a summary of the whole process.

The printed material and packaging teams were busy at work as well. They put together their respective teams, selected their projects, and submitted the worksheets seen in Figures 3-5 and 3-6. Clearly, both teams took on projects that had a tremendous ability to be leveraged over a substantially higher volume. It would be good to review these worksheets to see the similarity as well as differences between the three teams at Anything Inc.

Figure 3-5. Goal specification worksheet for printed manuals.

AIM & DRIVE: Agreeing to Manage Costs

Primary Cost: Pinted Manual

Total Spend: $9,790,000

Leverageable Spend: $102,760,000

Rationale for Choosing Primary Cost:
Team is very committed to managing this cost
Amount spent is well over the hurdle amount
The strategies can be leveraged across manuals for other products at Anything Inc.
Significant opportunities for cost reduction in the short term

---

Goals for Anything Inc.:

Finance	Achieve a 5% profit margin
Marketing	Increase market share of Zigmos by 6%
Marketing	Maintain aesthetic value of the current manual
Quality	Ensure that the manual is durable and can outlive the product
Procurement	Obtain lower price for manuals
Logistics	Lower weight/size of manuals
Customer service	To have the manual in different languages based on customer demographics

---

Supplier Goals:

Finance	Achieve a 12% net profit margin
Marketing	Total customer satisfaction
Logistics	Central distribution hubs
Quality	Maintain high quality of product at competitive prices
Production	Reduce number of colors
Production	Fewer languages
Production	Better volume forecasts

Figure 3-6. Goal specification worksheet for corrugated packaging.

AIM & DRIVE: Agreeing to Manage Costs

Primary Cost:	Corrugated Boxes for Zigmos

Total Spend: $2,475,000
Volume: 1,100,000
Leverageable Spend: $49,500,000

Rationale for Choosing Primary Cost:
This packaging is similar to other boxes used at Anything Inc.
Team is keen to learn this process and use leverage the ideas
Supplier is very cooperative and willing to work on breakthrough ideas

---

Goals for Anything Inc.:

Procurement	Reduce TCO by 8%
Procurement	Reduce purchase price by 15%
Procurement	Leverage procurement of corrugated boxes
Manufacturing	Avoid shut-down due to lack of packaging material
Manufacturing	Cope with wild uncertainty in business growth/shrinkage and technology changes
Manufacturing	On call help 24/7/365
Finance	Reduce inventory by 90%
Finance	Ensure lowest market price for boxes
Distribution	Reduce delivery time from 24 to 8 hrs
Distribution	To be environmentally responsible

Supplier Goals:

Sales	More direct contact with other Anything Inc. divisions
Design	Have access to Anything Inc. engineers for better concurrent engineering
Design	Continue to have input for graphic design
Finance	Realize net profit margin of 15%
Logistics	Reduce inventory by 50%

Checklist for Step 1: Agreeing on the Need to Manage Costs

❑ Review business plan and procurement/marketing strategy.

❑ Identify initial participants for the team.

❑ Agree on the primary cost or project topic for AIM & DRIVE.

❑ Select the rest of the cost management team, including stakeholders and supplier/s.

❑ Determine team goals from various perspectives.

❑ Complete the Goal Specification Worksheet.

❑ Update the Master Worksheet.

Identifying Critical Costs
in the Supply Chain

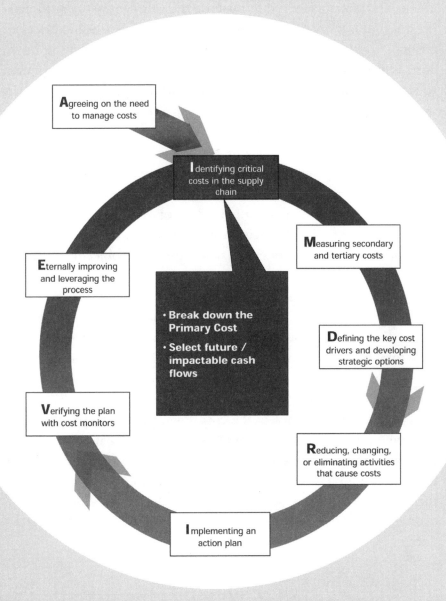

On October 21, 1993, the *Wall Street Journal* published an article by the don of business management, the late Dr. Peter F. Drucker, titled "The Five Deadly Business Sins." One of the deadly sins Dr. Drucker mentions is *cost-driven pricing*. According to him, the "only thing that works is price-driven costing. Most American and practically all European companies arrive at their prices by adding up costs and then putting a profit margin on top." He then adds: "If Toyota and Nissan succeed in pushing the German luxury auto makers out of the US market, it will be the result of their using price-led costing. To be sure, to start out with price and then whittle down costs is more work *initially*. But in the end, it is much less work than to start out wrong and then spend loss-making years bringing costs into line—let alone far cheaper than losing a market." Amen! Couldn't agree with you more, Dr. Drucker.

As global competition sets fire to the seats of top management in many companies, there is going to be a scramble to lower prices *at any cost*. And that is precisely what we want to avoid. The AIM & DRIVE process is designed to help develop a strategy of managing costs through the supply chain. A strategy driven by both customers and suppliers alike. A strategy that has one clear objective: to bring products with world-class quality and leading technology, on time, every time, at the lowest market price to the ultimate customer. This is the customer who is the *only* one who puts money into the value chain. The rules of economics are crystal clear: If total revenue is less than total cost, the firm will lose money. If this continues over a period of time, it is highly likely that firm will cease to exist as a business entity.

Figure 4-1 takes a look at the cost flow through the supply chain. It is the entire supply chain that ends with the ultimate consumer of the goods and services provided by the chain. How unfortunate it is that the traditional role of customer and supplier pits one against the other on the issue of price. If we all started with the common

Figure 4-1. Supply chain cost flow.

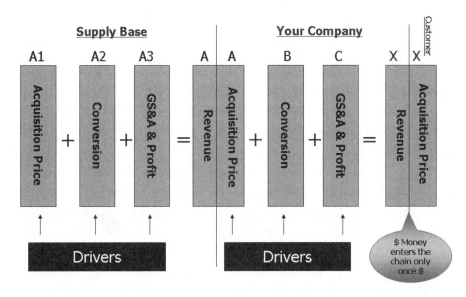

understanding that "costs" have to be reduced rather than just the price, I am convinced the relationship will start on a much better footing. And it will continue to build as the benefits of true cost management are shared through the supply chain.

In Figure 4-1, assume that your company is the final assembler of a consumer item that is sold to the end customer. The supply base represents your suppliers and their suppliers and so on. Let's pick up the action when a customer buys your product. To the customer, the amount paid for the item is the "acquisition price." To you, this represents revenue. The sum of all the "acquisition prices" paid by your customer base is your total revenue. Agreed? Now what is the basic economic formula for total revenue? It is:

$$\text{total revenue} = \text{total cost} \pm \text{profit/loss}$$

I believe we need to modify the basic formula for total cost and include profit as a cost element. The reason is that profit should be given the respect it deserves. As a company budgets for advertising, research and development, training, and management, so should it budget for a return on investment in the form of profit. This is a symbolic gesture but it is worth making in order to show a supplier that, as a customer, you do not expect it to run a charity.

Let's say a company has a total revenue of "$X." What is the breakdown of this total revenue? It's the sum of the acquisition price paid by the company to all its suppliers (we'll call that "A"), plus the conversion costs incurred by that company (call it "B"), and the administrative, marketing, and distribution costs needed to bring the product to its customer, plus or minus a profit or loss ("C"). Now, what if one had to further break down the acquisition price, "A"? Well, can you see something emerging from this model? And not surprisingly, it is the total revenue (total cost) of the next level supplier in a particular supply chain.

At this stage there appears to be a conflict of interest. If, for example, the team at Anything Inc. wanted to reduce its cost of Customer Service, one possible solution would be to find a way to negotiate the hourly rate of the Fixit technical service engineers and other billable personnel. Other things being equal, that action would reduce the *acquisition price* paid by Anything Inc. to Fixit. However, Fixit would see this as a drop in revenue from the Anything Inc. account. In situations like these a customer wants to reduce its acquisition price, A, in order to increase its profit margin, or to sustain a fall in the market price of its product without compromising on profit margin. On the other hand, the supplier would prefer to increase its revenue, A, by increasing the price charged to the customer. Unless the drop in price is offset by a change in volume, you are going to have a very disappointed source of supply. A firm that will compromise in some way on quality, delivery, or service. Or one that will eventually walk away from your business. It's a tough call when one gets down to face-to-face negotiations with a supplier. Should you go after the price at any cost? Isn't that what management is going to measure the team on, after all? Or will the team stand tall and take a strategic view?

Here's an example of an opening remark by Ms. Cheep of Anything Inc. to the account manager of one of Anything's major material suppliers: "Look Joe, this is the position. I'm under tremendous pressure from my management to lower the cost of direct material. It's now nearly 50 percent of our product selling price. With our customer becoming more informed and demanding, we have no alternative but to meet, and beat, the competition on price. Toward this end, we need to set a target of reducing the price we pay for your product or service by 15 percent per year for the next three years. Now, I could threaten you with moving the business or use other bullying tactics to extract price concessions. But, I'm not going to stoop to that level. I'd like to work with you to identify costs at your end. That means we need to understand your acquisition price (A1), your conversion costs (A2), and your administrative, marketing, and distribution costs (A3). Then, we can see what action we can take to reduce or eliminate some of those costs. You will be able to reduce your price without compromising your margins by much. In fact, with your experience, you may be able to help me identify costs in my conversion process that I could reduce. Of course, you may consider this to be proprietary, against your company policy or whatever. In that case, I will still pursue my goal of price reduction and leave it to you to manage your costs as you see fit. The choice is yours."

Firm but fair, isn't it? The question is how long can a company continue to slash costs as a reaction to competitive price pressure? Isn't it time for someone to lead the way? There has to be a more strategic focus to cost management. Look at Figure 4-1 again. If a team wants to tackle the costs of incoming material (the acquisition price), it needs to follow the same process as it did with its customer. That is, for the acquisition price to drop, the total cost of the supply base has to decrease. Therefore, we'll need to identify costs regardless of who incurs them. That means we have to sit down with a cross-functional team, including key suppliers or customers where necessary, agree on the need to manage costs, and begin Step 2 of the AIM & DRIVE process: identifying critical costs in the supply chain.

Map the Process

Once a cost management strategy team has been assembled it is important that everyone view the process before, during, and after their respective activities are performed. Process mapping for the purpose of writing a cost management strategy doesn't have to be very sophisticated. All we are trying to accomplish is to view costs and activities from different perspectives. It also helps the participants understand the elements of costs for each activity. A rule of thumb would be to keep the initial process map to around ten to fifteen activity "boxes." If needed, one or two key boxes could be expanded into separate process flow diagrams.

Before breaking down the cost of customer service, the team at Anything Inc. developed a process map, which is illustrated in Figure 4-2. Having done that, they talked in general terms about the type of cost elements that would describe the activities in each activity box. This does not have to follow any ledger account heads or, for that matter, generally accepted accounting principles. The terminology is not important at this stage. I call it the "Windows" system. Just choose a name for the activity, as if you were naming a file. Then, look at the list of names; determine whether some of them could be "filed" under the same "folder" or "subfolder." For example, the predominant cost incurred in activity box #1 is labor charges for the customer service center operator, a cost that is fairly administrative in nature. In activity box #2, it is again a labor cost but this time of a technical

Figure 4-2. Process map for customer service for goods under warranty.

THE PROCESS MAP

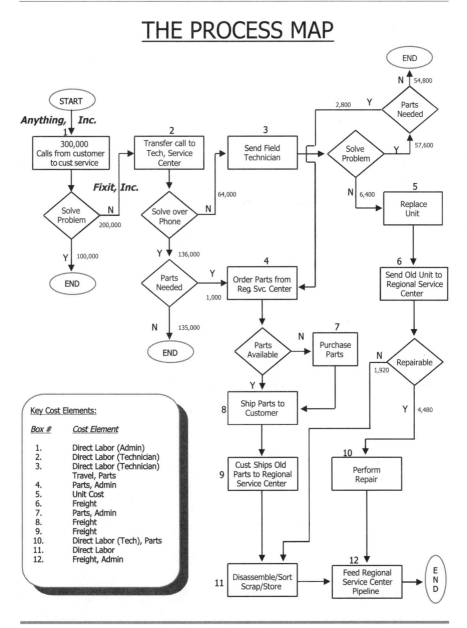

Key Cost Elements:

Box #	Cost Element
1.	Direct Labor (Admin)
2.	Direct Labor (Technician)
3.	Direct Labor (Technician) Travel, Parts
4.	Parts, Admin
5.	Unit Cost
6.	Freight
7.	Parts, Admin
8.	Freight
9.	Freight
10.	Direct Labor (Tech), Parts
11.	Direct Labor
12.	Freight, Admin

service center person who is a more highly skilled individual. Next, in activity box #3 you have a field service technician's labor cost but also the cost of travel to get to the customer's site and, perhaps, some parts to perform the repair, if necessary. Thus, for these three activity boxes you could have about five cost elements that stand out. A team may decide to look at all of them separately or take the three labor categories and put them under a general category (a file folder like in Windows) called LABOR COST. Following the trail of cost categories, the *primary cost* would be the cost of customer service, a *secondary* or second-level cost would be direct labor and a *tertiary* or third-level cost would be Technical Service Center (TSC) labor. At this stage, depending on the level of cost knowledge or cost cooperation by a supplier, the team may take a stab at estimating the cost of each of the major activity boxes. Alternatively, if it is the acquisition price that is being discussed, the team could break that cost into the typical five key cost elements or "subfolders," namely:

1. Direct material
2. Direct labor
3. Manufacturing or service overhead
4. General, selling, administration, and distribution
5. Profit

It is up to the team to determine how deep they would like to drill down into the subcost elements. Sometimes you may break a certain cost into subcost elements and then decide that it does not add any value doing that. There is no hard-and-fast rule as to how deep you have to go.

Select Critical Costs to be Managed

Once the team has identified the topic, established its goals from different perspectives, completed the Goal Specification Worksheet, mapped the process, and understood the general cost elements associated with each cost activity, it is time to begin the process of identifying critical costs in the supply chain. Remember, so far, no numbers have been attributed to the cost elements identified in the process map. It's time to take a stab at that. A good guide is the Cost Activity Worksheet (Figure 4-3) that was developed by Steve Frels and his Strategic Supply Management Services team at Deere and Company. The purpose is not to fill in every single item on the worksheet, but to start from the left and move toward the right *only* if the team recognizes the cost to be significant in monetary terms, as a percentage of the total, or if it happens to have a major variance from the budget. Also, it is not that important to be exact with your numbers. I've always maintained, "it's better to be approximately correct than to be exactly wrong."

Compare Figures 4-1 and 4-3. See the similarity? In Figure 4-3, if you are looking at it from a customer's perspective, the bottom line is the sales price/revenue. This is "X" in Figure 4-1. The Direct Material box represents "A" in Figure 4-1. Direct Labor, Manufacturing, and Engineering Overhead are the equivalent of Conversion Costs ("B") in Figure 4-1. And GS&A and Profit & Others in Figure 4-3 correspond to "C" in Figure 4-1. If you were to go further, then you could do a similar Cost Activity Worksheet for the supply base where Direct Material becomes the bottom line for the supplier (we'll use "A" instead of "X"). The rest is the same, except "A1" replaces "A," "A2" for "B," and "A3" for "C."

Obtaining Cost Data

As a team begins filling in the Cost Activity Worksheet for a product or service, the first signs of trouble emerge. While it may be possible to estimate some of the costs, there are times when the customer has no clue whatsoever about the suppliers' cost structure. I am often

(text continues on page 66)

Figure 4-3. Cost activity worksheet for Anything Inc.

Category	$	Group	$	Cost Activity	$
Direct Material	150	Direct Material		Purchased unit price Freight and transportation (inbound) Customs, duties, foreign currency exchange	
Direct Labor	15	Direct Labor		Direct labor Direct labor benefits and allowances	
Manufacturing Overhead	45	Machine and Process Costs		Depreciation (equipment) Maintenance (equipment) Process costs (electricity, gas, water, etc.) Process materials (paint, weld, adhesives, etc.) Production supplies	
		Material Handling		Receiving Movement (through manufacturing) Storage Shipping	
		Quality Costs		Appraisal (audit/inspection) Rework (repair) Scrap and yield losses Warranty and returned goods	
		Tooling Costs (dies, fixtures, etc.)		Depreciation (tooling) Maintenance (tooling) Perishable tools and tool sets Purchased part tooling	
		Facility Costs (buildings)		Receiving Manufacturing Shipping/warehousing	

Engineering Overhead	75	Management Costs		Forecasting, order placement, expediting Data documentation/administration Inventory management Manufacturing information systems Manufacturing supervision Production control Supply management	
			25	Design engineering (manufacture, quality, etc.) Materials engineering (selection, etc.) Process engineering Product research and development; test	
General, Selling & Administrative (GS&A)		General and Administrative Costs	25	Corporate expenses Accounting, legal, H.R., etc. Training Travel Other	
		Selling and Distribution Costs	50	Packaging, freight and transportation Market development (advertising, promo, etc.) Order processing (customer) Warranty, sales and service support (customer) Distribution costs (receive, store, ship, etc.) Other	6 30 1 10 2 1
Profit & Other	15			Financing costs (interest) Pre-tax profit Other	
Total	300				

Adapted from worksheet by Steve Frels and others of Deere & Company.

asked: "Will the supplier share such sensitive data"? My first response is with another question: "Have you asked for it?" You will be amazed at the amount of data a customer can gather by simply asking the right question of the right supplier with the right objective in mind. Here are three ways that will help extract vital cost information about a product or service:

1. *Supplier-Provided Data.* In order to obtain cost information from a supplier, the customer should take the time to prepare a well-thought-out Request for Quotation (RFQ) that includes, among other information, a detailed breakdown of the supplier's quoted price. The objective should be clear and communicated. The customer is trying to *understand* the supplier's quotation better and not attempting to be an auditor. Many times, one or two suppliers will not provide data but others will. As long as the prices are within a reasonable range, a customer can create an average price profile from the cooperative suppliers to estimate the cost structure of the non-cooperative ones. Here, it must be made clear that under *no* circumstances should the buyer share the specific numbers of one supplier with another. To do so would be unethical and while it may buy the buyer some short-term benefit, the long-term consequences would be disastrous.

What if a supplier does not provide a cost breakdown in response to an RFQ? A customer must be persistent. Of course, the first reaction of a supplier to such a request is bound to be, "why do they want this information?" Or, "it is against our policy to share such information with a customer." I remember a story narrated to me by Bob, the Director of Electronics Marketing at a major U.S. company. He was approached by one of his account managers with an RFQ from a Japanese auto company that had just established a plant in the United States and wanted to source a small electronic device locally. The RFQ included a form with a fairly detailed cost breakdown expected of the supplier. Bob's initial reaction was, "We do not give out such data.

Just enter the price at the bottom and send it back to them." A couple of days later, the account representative came into Bob's office with a FedEx package containing the same RFQ with a little note attached to it. It was from the category manager for electronic parts who wrote: "Thanks for your very interesting quote. However, it appears you forgot to include the breakdown of the quote on the worksheet attached to the RFQ. Please fill this in and send it back to us at your earliest convenience so that we can process your quotation." Bob scribbled a note on a Post-it pad and sent it back to the customer. The note simply said: "We do not share this type of data with anyone." Two days later the documents came back by FedEx with another short note, also on a Post-it pad, with the words, "We are sorry that you think of us as *anyone*. We would like to work with valued partner suppliers who think of us as *someone special*." The package included the customer's Supplier Relationship Management program and its vision of being one of the largest manufacturers of automobiles in the United States within the next ten years. Bob and his team met to discuss what could be a future strategic account and decided to make an exception. Not only was the quotation successful, but the customer used the cost data to engage with this supplier to find ways to take costs down further that resulted in a 25 percent reduction in the part price within a year. Ten years later, as Bob pointed out, the Japanese automaker was, indeed, one of the largest manufacturers in the United States and Bob's company was one of its largest suppliers of electronic parts. Persistence paid off in this case.

2. *Development of "Should Cost" Models.* Despite all the persistence in the world, there are times when suppliers are still not willing to share cost data. At such times it is immensely useful for the customer to break the ice by developing a should cost model for the product or service being purchased. The level of detail in the model can vary from an industry cost profile to a detailed process-based model. Before developing a detailed model a team should think about

its objective. Is it necessary to establish what the product should cost or is the team satisfied with the price but wants to better understand the breakdown of that price into its various cost elements? The concept and process of Should Cost Modeling can be found in the book *Zero Base Pricing*™: *Achieving World Class Competitiveness through Reduced All-in-Costs,* by Burt, Norquist, and Anklesaria (Probus Publishing, 1990). Figure 4-4 shows the progression in level of detail obtained from cost models.

3. *Availability of Internal Data.* In some cases a company may have had experience in producing a particular product or service and have now decided to outsource it. In such cases, it helps to dig out

Figure 4-4. Should cost model phases.

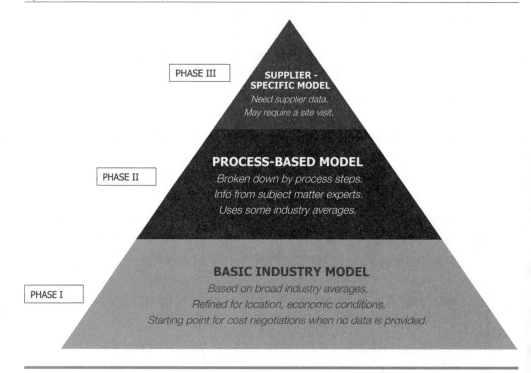

the cost data from the customer's internal records and use that as a base for estimating the cost breakdown of the supplier's quote. While the numbers may not match exactly, one could assume that the percentages are fairly similar.

The purpose of developing a cost breakdown for use in the AIM & DRIVE process is to *understand* the cost structure of a supplier's price and be able to *identify* critical costs in the supply chain. Notice the words "supply chain." I have often observed that when teams consisting of two or more levels of the supply chain engage in an AIM & DRIVE exercise, the first thing the customer wants to do is tear down the supplier's price. That *may* be fine, provided the team has determined that the acquisition price is one of the critical costs in the supply chain. In order to do this, it is necessary to lay out *all* costs associated with the target product or service. And, that can be a nightmare. The Total Cost of Ownership (TCO) is the present value of all costs incurred during the life of a product or service. In the AIM & DRIVE process, unlike for a make-versus-buy analysis, it is not necessary to estimate the present value of each cost element. However, it is important to at least identify the in-house costs that a customer incurs in addition to the acquisition of the product or service.

Figure 4-5 illustrates the type of cost elements in each of the TCO categories. The team needs to prepare a list of costs in each category, estimate the values of those costs, and identify which of those costs are *critical* in the supply chain. Most often, a customer has poor or nonexistent data on the cost of receiving, inspection, storage, handling, scrap, warranties, field service, lost productivity or lost sales, outbound logistics, customer returns, and end-of-life costs. So, it is easier to focus on the supplier's price. That is a big mistake. Not that the supplier's price is not important. It's just that there are so many opportunities when one looks internally as well. It is hard to calculate some of the costs in the Total Cost of Ownership model. For example,

Figure 4-5. Example of cost elements in the total cost of ownership.

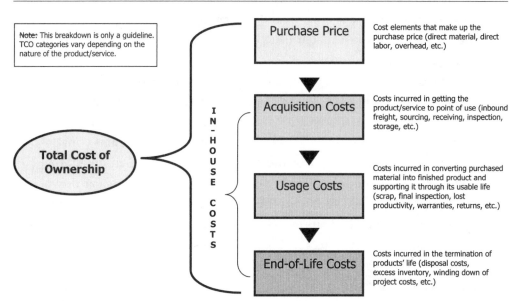

the cost of lost sales or lost productivity may be difficult to estimate. If the team determines that it is a critical cost to consider, an effort must be made to put a number on that type of cost.

The team at Anything Inc. working on Customer Service looked at the process map and determined that they would break down the primary cost into the following second-tier (L2) costs:

- Direct labor
- Direct materials (spare parts and finished units)
- Logistics
- Administration charges

These costs are summarized in a worksheet, shown in Figure 4-6.

At this stage the team may decide that one or more of the second-

Figure 4-6. Estimated cost of customer service for goods under warranty.

AIM & DRIVE: Identifying Critical Costs							
PRIMARY COST : CUSTOMER SERVICE FOR GOODS UNDER WARRANTY							
	L2	L3	L2	L3	Future Cash Flow	Impactable	Select
$21,813,640	94.0%		Labor costs				
$696,180	3.0%		Direct Material (parts)				
$464,120	2.0%		Logistics				
$232,060	1.0%		Administration				
$23,206,000	100.0%		Primary Cost Total				

ary costs could be broken down even further. This would create a third-level or *tertiary* cost (L3). For example, direct labor may be broken down into technical labor, field service labor, and repair shop labor. Likewise, logistics could be broken down into freight, inventory, and handling costs. It is not mandatory that all costs be broken down into smaller elements. This depends on the team and the project chosen. At the cost of repetition, the purpose of a cost breakdown is to *identify critical costs* in the supply chain, not to audit the price structure of a supplier. The definition of the term *critical* is left to the members of the team. In some cases the choice would be made going purely by the numbers. Take the top two or three dollar items and break them down further. In other cases, teams have chosen costs that they believe could be leveraged across other projects or across the entire enterprise, even though they are not of significant value in the current project. A classic example in the case of the Anything Inc. team is the choice of logistics as a cost worth breaking down further.

Figure 4-7 illustrates the discussion above. Having broken down

Figure 4-7. Completed worksheet for identifying the critical costs of customer service for goods under warranty.

AIM & DRIVE: Identifying Critical Costs								
PRIMARY COST : CUSTOMER SERVICE FOR GOODS UNDER WARRANTY								
		L2	L3	L2	L3	Future Cash Flow	Impactable	Select
$21,813,640		94.0%		Labor costs				
	$2,320,600		10.0%		Service Center	Y	Y	
	$19,028,920		82.0%		Field Service	Y	Y	Y
	$464,120		2.0%		Repair	Y	Y	
$696,180		3.0%		Direct Material (parts)		Y	Y	Y
$464,120		2.0%		Logistics				
	$232,060		1.0%		Freight	Y	Y	Y
	$116,030		0.5%		Handling	Y	Y	
	$116,030		0.5%		Inventory	Y	Y	
$232,060		1.0%		Administration		Y	N	
$23,206,000		100.0%		Primary Cost Total				

direct labor and logistics costs, the next decision is which of these costs are critical enough to carry forward to the next step in the AIM & DRIVE process. The decision to further break down a certain cost is based on a "yes" answer to each of the following two questions:

1. Is the cost a future cash flow?
2. Is this a cost that a team can impact?

In the first question the objective is to write a strategy for costs that is likely to be incurred in the future. If the cost is a nonrecurring cost (one-time cost), then it may still make sense to write a strategy provided that the one-time expense has not yet been incurred (it is to be incurred in the future). Nonrecurring expenses, for example, include purchase of capital equipment, tooling, development, and buildings. If a piece of equipment or tooling is to be purchased in the near future, you may be interested in writing a strategy *before* spending the money.

However, the team is most clearly interested in *recurring* future costs. Examples of recurring costs are material, labor, freight, and administration. Having selected certain cost elements that are recurring future cash flows, the next question is whether or not the team is able to impact the selected cost. Sometimes the cost may be mandated by a government body (example: property taxes, license fees, environmental cleanup fees), which a team has little or no control over. This cost element will be dropped from further discussion. In other cases the cost may be impactable, but this team is not in a position to do so. In such cases, a team would pass on its suggestion to another team to develop a strategy for this cost element. In Figure 4-7 the team at Anything Inc. argues that with the exception of administration costs, all other costs were future cash flows that were impactable by the team. Administrative costs were shared with other functions of the company, allocated by the corporate office, and thus beyond the control of their team. So they set aside administration costs for now, entered direct labor, direct materials, and freight in column "I" of their Master Worksheet (Figure 4-8), and proceeded to the next step of the AIM & DRIVE process: measuring secondary and tertiary costs.

The two other teams at Anything Inc. went through the same process to select their critical costs to carry over to the next step of the process. The Printed Manual team spent about $9.8 million on the set of manuals that accompanied each Zigmo. There were three manuals per Zigmo: a Quick Start Guide of 70 pages, an Operating Guide of 194 pages, and a Personal Information Guide of 223 pages. They decided to break down the primary cost of Printed Manuals into second-tier costs of design, paper, printing, and translation. This breakdown and the cost elements chosen by that team to be carried forward to the next step are illustrated in Figure 4-9.

The Corrugated Boxes team took a different approach and broke the cost per box into two major subcategories: manufacturing and distribution. They then went all the way down to level five for manu-

Figure 4-8. Master worksheet for customer service for goods under warranty.

AIM & DRIVE: Master Worksheet

A PRIMARY COST : CUSTOMER SERVICE FOR GOODS UNDER WARRANTY

Total Spend = $23,206,000

CRITICAL COSTS	COST DRIVERS	KEY COST DRIVERS	SELECTED STRATEGY STATEMENT	ACTION ITEMS	WHO	DUE DATE
I	M	D	R	I	VE	VE
Field service labor (82%)						
Direct material (3%)						
Freight (1%)						

Figure 4-9. Completed worksheet for identifying the critical costs of printed manuals.

AIM & DRIVE: Identifying Critical Costs							
PRIMARY COST : PRINTED MANUALS							
	L2	L3	L2	L3	Future Cash Flow	Impactable	Select
$391,600	4.0%		Design				
$391,600		4.0%	Labor		Y	Y	Y
			Overhead		Y		
$8,223,600	84.0%		Direct Materials (Paper)		Y	Y	Y
$979,000	10.0%		Printing		Y	Y	Y
$195,800	2.0%		Translation		Y	Y	Y
$9,790,000	100.0%		Primary Cost Total				

facturing and level four for distribution costs. Take a look at this in Figure 4-10. Having seen three totally different cost breakdowns I hope you realize that it is up to each team to determine how they want to break down the primary cost and whether to use a per unit cost or the total cost.

Figure 4-10. Completed worksheet for identifying the critical costs of corrugated boxes.

AIM & DRIVE : Identifying Critical Costs

PRIMARY COST : CORRUGATED BOXES

		L2	L3	L4	L5	L2	L3	L4	L5	Future Cash Flow	Impactable	Select
$1.47		65.3%				**Manufacturing**						
	$0.08		3.6%				Prepress & Setup					
	$0.85		37.8%				Corrugated & Box Manufacturing					
		$0.73		32.4%				Board				
		$0.12		5.3%				Others				
	$0.38		16.9%				Production					
		$0.28		12.4%				Others				
									Processing Costs			
		$0.10		4.4%				Pallets				
	$0.04		1.8%				Freight			Y	Y	
	$0.12		5.3%				Profit			Y	Y	Y
$0.78		34.7%				**Distribution**						
	$0.17		7.6%				Inbound Freight			Y	Y	
	$0.28		12.4%				Variable Plant			Y	Y	
		$0.17		7.6%				Rent		Y	N	Y
		$0.09		4.0%				Labor				
		$0.02		0.9%				Others				
	$0.27		12.0%				GSDA			Y	Y	
	$0.02		0.9%				Outbound Freight					
	$0.04		1.8%				Profit					
$2.25		100.0%				Primary Cost Total						

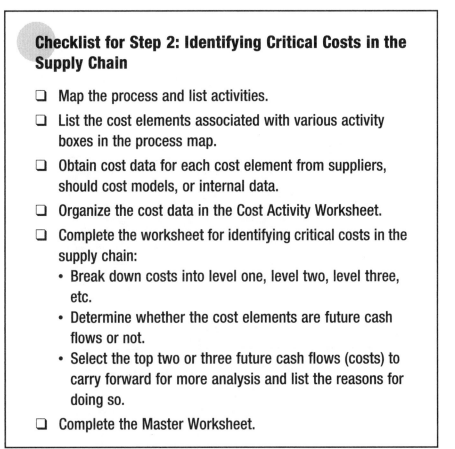

Checklist for Step 2: Identifying Critical Costs in the Supply Chain

❑ Map the process and list activities.

❑ List the cost elements associated with various activity boxes in the process map.

❑ Obtain cost data for each cost element from suppliers, should cost models, or internal data.

❑ Organize the cost data in the Cost Activity Worksheet.

❑ Complete the worksheet for identifying critical costs in the supply chain:
  • Break down costs into level one, level two, level three, etc.
  • Determine whether the cost elements are future cash flows or not.
  • Select the top two or three future cash flows (costs) to carry forward for more analysis and list the reasons for doing so.

❑ Complete the Master Worksheet.

## CHAPTER 5

Measuring Secondary and Tertiary Costs

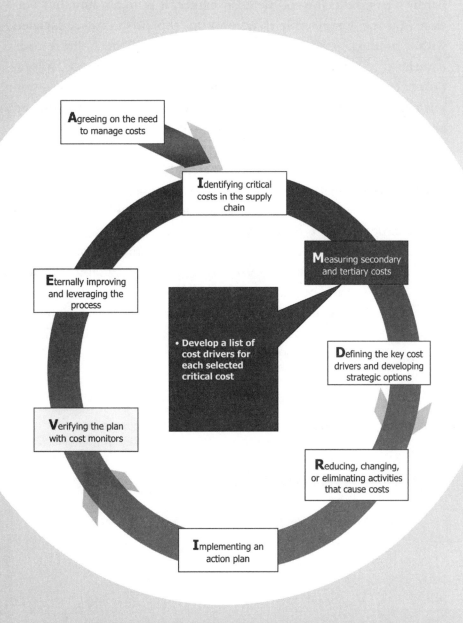

A cost that is not measured will rarely be managed. One of the reasons why cost management, unlike Total Quality Management, has not been successfully implemented by more firms is that it is so difficult to measure many of the critical costs in the supply chain. Further, users of cost data are aware that if and when they get cost information through existing cost accounting methods, the data is hardly a true reflection of the cost. Rather, it is an accountant's version. You see, it's possible to account for the direct costs associated with a product or service. But when it comes to the indirect costs (overhead) that's when everything just goes "over your head." Allocation of overhead has been something that has obsessed the accounting profession for decades. No matter which method of overhead allocation you use, you are bound to make one person or the other mad.

The first thing that a cost management team has to realize is that different companies use different cost accounting methods. Trying to determine which system is best is not going to help anyone. And costs, particularly overhead costs, do not go away by arguing about which method of allocation is correct, and how the allocation needs to be made. Yet, I constantly see customers trying to analyze the supplier's overhead and protesting about the overhead rate. What a waste of energy! Look, you are not going to change the way a company allocates its costs. Why don't you focus, instead, on reducing or eliminating real overhead costs?

Methods of Measuring Costs

Cost accounting systems can be broken into two categories:

1. Allocation-based systems
2. Management-based systems

Let's take a brief look at these two types of systems.

Allocation-Based Systems

Allocation-based systems are those accounting systems that attempt to allocate costs to product or service centers using either traditional or modern methods of cost accounting. Traditional cost accounting systems include *job costing, process costing,* and *standard costing.* Examples of modern cost accounting systems would be *activity-based costing* (ABC) and *process-based costing* (PBC).

Under a *job-costing* system, direct costs like raw material and direct labor are charged to specific jobs based on usage of materials and labor. People working on specific jobs are made to fill in job cards, and the raw material drawn for a particular job is charged on the same card. An example of this process would be to take a look at your last auto repair bill. Notice how each department filled out a section showing exactly what parts were used on your car. Then the various labor hours for each operation were entered and a labor rate used to convert the hours into dollars. This labor rate is a *loaded* rate. That means the rate includes the wages paid to the repair technician as well as an "allocation" of indirect costs like supervision, tools, space, utilities, depreciation of equipment, management, and so on. So now you understand why a kid with a high school degree, working on your car, is charged out at $50 plus per hour. Job costing is used by consultants, lawyers, construction companies, and advertising agencies, to name a few.

Process costing is a system where costs are assigned to identical products that are produced in a continuous flow through a series of manufacturing processes. Each step of the process is like a *job.* For example, in the auto industry there are a series of assembly operations, followed by processes like painting, finishing, and transporting to dealers. Overhead is allocated as a percentage of direct labor at each step of the process. The main purpose of process costing is to calculate the value of inventory of raw materials, work-in-process, and finished goods based on what accountants call *equivalent units*. Does it help in reducing costs? Probably not.

Standard costing is a system where target costs are set for both material and labor. A target cost is a cost that is reasonably required to achieve a given objective under specified conditions. Who sets the targets and are they accurate? That, I'm afraid, will remain an eternal secret. I remember a cost estimator of a very famous, multinational corporation, who told me the secret formula in developing a standard cost. According to this person the first step is to pull in data from a whole bunch of sources. Once the data is gathered, you multiply each number by zero and add the number you want your standard cost to be. Now, I really hope that this is not true. But then . . . why do you have that smile on your face? Because you know that sometimes it *is* the way standards are established, isn't it?

Under the traditional costing systems, overhead costs are usually allocated on the basis of direct labor. It is apparent that allocating costs on a single base is not only unrealistic, it is unfair. In the 1980s, activity-based costing (ABC) entered the field along with the Total Quality Management (TQM) process.

Activity-based costing can best be described as a system that assigns the costs to products based on the causal relationships of the activities required to produce the product. According to CAM-I, a professional standards organization for accounting, "activity-based accounting is a collection of financial and operational performance information dealing with significant activities of the business. Activities represent repetitive tasks performed by each specialized group within a company as it executes its business objectives."

To put it in a layperson's terms, ABC seeks to allocate overhead costs by using many "bases" instead of just direct labor, machine hours, or square footage. As described in the definition, costs are allocated to product lines based on the "activities" required or "consumed" by a product line. Originally used by companies like John

Deere, Hewlett-Packard, and Harley-Davidson, ABC has gained world-wide recognition as a system that induces positive behavior. Unfortunately, it is still a system of allocation, albeit a more sophisticated one.

There are many who feel that ABC systems do not focus on overall business processes. So in the early 1990s a new school of cost accounting emerged to take issue with the drawbacks of ABC. Proponents of this system focused on the fact that all activities belonged to processes and thus developed a system of cost accounting called *process-based costing* (PBC). To be quite honest, there's very little difference between ABC and PBC, except that PBC forces companies to draw process maps to chart the flow of activities through organizations. Costs are traced to each activity in the process. In other words, PBC provides an overall framework within which ABC fits. But just like ABC, PBC is a sophisticated allocation system.

Management-Based Systems

You may have observed from the previous discussion that ABC systems are designed for the factories of the future. They seek to identify the *causes* of overhead and thereby influence behavior. However, having worked with many companies that have implemented ABC systems, there seems to be a trace of disillusionment amongst users of the system. I have been told that the system is growing more and more complex, leaving the users of data more confused than they had been with traditional cost accounting methods.

It would be easy to throw in the towel, except for the fact that if we don't find a way to measure costs, we will find it really difficult to manage them. The time has come to turn to our last resort—common sense. I believe that ultimately the "ten-meter managers" in the cost management team will be able to measure costs far more realistically than any accounting system, provided, of course, that we allow them to do so. Would you rather have information that is "approximately right"? Or would you rather it is "exactly wrong"? It's time to give common sense a chance. Formula-based costing is a commonsense process where algebraic formulas are used to measure costs, define cost drivers, and develop strategic options to reduce, change, or eliminate activities that cause costs.

Understanding Variables

In order to understand the basis of Formula-based costing we may have to make a trip down memory lane to your first algebra class. I remember when my fifth-grade teacher, Mrs. D'Souza, explained the concept of variables. "Mark," she asked my classmate, "if x is a number that is equal to the product of three other numbers, a, b, and c. And if $a = 1$, $b = 2$, and $c = 3$, what is the value of x?"

Without much trouble, Mark figured out that $1 \times 2 \times 3$ was equal to 6. So he replied: "The value of x is equal to 6." Mrs. D'Souza said, "Great job, Mark," and he sat down with a big smile on his round face.

Next Mrs. D'Souza asked another classmate of mine, Lester, to stand up. She said, "Lester, if x is a number equal to the product of three other numbers, a, b, and c. And if $a = 2$, $b = 3$, and $c = 4$, what is the value of x?" Lester replied immediately, "The value of x is equal to 24, Mrs. D'Souza." Like Mark, Lester was complimented and took his seat.

By now, I was totally confused. How could the same letter, x, be equal to 6 and also be equal to 24? I knew my numbers enough to know that if I went to a store and asked for six pieces of candy there was no way I would receive twenty-four. And vice-versa, if I paid for twenty-four candies and received six, no one in the world would be able to convince me that it was the same. So, I raised my hand and asked Mrs. D'Souza how x could be two different numbers. That's when I learned the meaning of the term "variable."

After complimenting me for the "good question," Mrs. D'Souza went on to explain that in an algebraic equation the left-hand side (LHS), x, represented the result or the solution. The elements on the right-hand side (RHS), a, b, and c, were variables. That is to say, these values varied within a certain range. In algebra we use the subscript i to represent the value of the lower limit and the superscript j to refer to the upper limit of the variable. For example, if a represented the percentage of parts rejected by the customer, then i (lower limit) would be equal to 0.00 and j would be 1.00 or 100 percent. So, depending on the given value of each variable (n), and the function sign between each of the variables, the outcome or result on the left-hand side would be different.

Three decades later I realized that in cost management, the LHS represented the "cost being measured" (the result). The variables on the RHS were nothing more than "cost drivers," since the value on the LHS depended on the respective values on the RHS. So a "cost driver" is a measure of an activity that "causes" a cost. Wow! That also means that the LHS is really a floating target since the "variables" by definition "vary" and are NOT constant. So here we are, spending all the time in the cost accounting world trying to put a number on every single cost element when, in fact, that number has changed even before the ink has dried on the report. Instead, we should be focusing on the current value of each driver, determining the best-in-class value and reviewing our options in order to move closer to the benchmark value.

Cause-and-Effect Relationship

You are given the following problem in your Algebra 101 class:

Company A has a manufacturing capacity of 1,000,000 units and is currently operating at 80 percent of capacity. If the company scraps 2 percent of its output and the cost per unit scrapped is $50, what is the cost of scrap generated?

In order to solve this problem you need to set up an equation. It would be something like this:

Let:

$x =$	cost of scrap generated	$= ?$
$a =$	manufacturing capacity in units	$= 1{,}000{,}000$
$b =$	actual capacity	$= 0.80$
$c =$	scrap rate	$= 0.02$
$d =$	cost per unit scrapped	$= \$50$

Solving for x:

$$x = a \times b \times c \times d$$

$$x = 1{,}000{,}000 \times 0.8 \times 0.02 \times 50$$

$$x = \$800{,}000$$

Now this is a really easy problem, but look what one can learn from it. First of all, the value of scrap is the *cost* being measured. The variables a, b, c, and d are the *drivers* since they *cause* the cost to be $\$800{,}000$ (or any other number). Any change in one or more of the variables will have an immediate *effect* on the LHS. Each of these drivers represents a value that changes within a range. For example, the drivers b and c are both percentages. So their lower limit would be 0 and the upper limit 1.00 (100 percent written as a number). The lower limit of the cost driver d would be 0 and the upper limit a positive number with a realistic ceiling depending on the product and the market.

Focusing on one of the drivers, say c, we need to ask the question, What determines the rate of scrap? In other words, What is the variable c a function of? A few factors that come to mind include skill of the operators, quality of raw material, type of equipment, number of setups, number of steps in the process, customer specifications/ tolerances, and so on. In the AIM & DRIVE terminology these functions are referred to as *strategic options*. Strategic options tell us ''how'' we may be able to affect a driver, which in turn would affect the cost we are trying to manage. We'll deal with that in the next chapter. For now, let's learn the secret of developing cost drivers for each critical cost in the supply chain.

Developing Cost Drivers in Formula-Based Costing

Figure 5-1 illustrates the fundamentals of Formula-Based Costing. Study it well. This could be the magic formula that opens the doors to a new way of thinking about measuring cost.

Figure 5-1. Understanding formula-based costing.

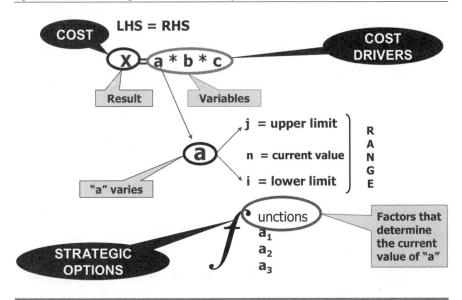

Points to Remember in Formula-Based Costing:

1. The logical end of a formula is the Revenue Driver. Sometimes it is hard for a team to determine where to stop stretching a formula. The general rule is that a formula should end with a revenue driver. In other words, what is the ultimate source of revenue for which this cost is being incurred?

2. There is only *one* Revenue Driver in a supply chain. Money enters the supply chain only once, so you should stretch the formula until the point where the ultimate customer pays for the product or service. While this is theoretically correct for measuring supply chain costs, it is sometimes more practical to end where money changes hands in a specific project instead of the entire supply chain.

3. A plus sign in a formula indicates Cost Elements, not Cost Drivers. You will notice that in the examples used earlier, the variables on the right-hand side of an equation have a multiplication sign between them. Why are there no plus or minus signs? The reason is that when plus or minus signs are introduced they represent subcost elements, and not Cost Drivers.

4. A Cost Element is a physical expense that can be expressed in currency over a specified period, usually a year.

5. A Cost Driver must be a numerically expressible variable. In order for the equation to be valid, all variables on the right-hand side *must* be quantifiable. You cannot take the wage rate, measured in dollars per hour, and multiply it by "skill of the operator." It just would not make sense.

6. A "qualitative" factor will always be a "function or strategic option." This is where "skill of the operator" would find a place, since the wage rate is a variable that is dependent, among other things, on the skill of the operator.

You may want to go back and read the list again. Make sure you really understand the definitions and how the elements interact before you move on in this chapter.

Writing a Formula for Each Secondary or Tertiary Cost

A useful hint in writing an algebraic formula for a cost element is to remember that all cost elements, by definition, should be measured in currency over a specific period. So, if the LHS is to equal the RHS, then the formula has to eventually be:

$$\frac{\$}{year} = \frac{\$}{year}$$

If the formula was for direct labor, the first step would be to expand the RHS so that:

$$\frac{\$}{year} = \frac{\$}{hour} \times \frac{hours}{year}$$

See how the hours cancel out to leave the RHS the same as the LHS? The secret, therefore, is to remember that the numerator of the next variable should be the same term as the denominator of the previous variable. This way, the equation continues to be in balance. The hours per year can be broken further into:

$$\frac{\#\ hours\ paid}{\#\ hours\ worked} \times \frac{\#\ hours\ worked}{year}$$

The formula would now read:

$$\frac{\$}{year} = \frac{\$}{hour} \times \frac{\#\ hours\ paid}{\#\ hours\ worked} \times \frac{\#\ hours\ worked}{year}$$

Depending on the process, the formula could be stretched to include the number of activities, the number of steps in each activity, and so on. A generic formula for labor would look something like this:

$$\frac{\$}{year} = \frac{\$}{hour} \times \frac{\#\ hours\ paid}{\#\ hours\ worked} \times \frac{\#hours\ worked}{step} \times \frac{\#\ steps}{activity} \times \frac{\#\ activities}{\#\ completed\ activities}$$

$$\times \frac{\#\ completed\ activities}{run} \times \frac{\#\ runs}{\#\ of\ units\ produced} \times \frac{\#\ of\ units\ produced}{\#\ units\ sold} \times \frac{\#\ units\ sold}{year}$$

This formula could be stretched a lot further depending on the process but this will do for now. Once a team is satisfied with the formula, the next step is to name each variable or cost driver. In the example above:

- The $ per hour is the *wage rate*.
- The number of hours paid per hours worked is the *labor utilization*.
- The number of hours worked per step is the *speed*.
- The number of steps per activity is the *process flow*.
- The number of activities per number of completed activities represents the *labor efficiency*.
- The number of completed activities per run is the *process requirement*.
- The number of runs per number of units produced shows the *run size*.

- The units produced per units sold would be the *planning efficiency*.

- The number of units sold per year is the *revenue driver*.

The ultimate formula can be tested for reasonableness by inserting actual numbers.

Back to our story. Remember that in Figure 4-7, the Customer Services team at Anything Inc. chose the following secondary/tertiary costs for further analysis:

- Direct labor (field service)

- Direct material (parts)

- Freight

The team then wrote a formula for each critical cost element identified, as you can see in Figure 5-2.

Notice how, for example, in writing the formula for field service labor, the team started with the lowest common measure of labor costs, the hourly wage represented by the dollars per hour. They then followed the process map to determine how long it took the technician to complete a field service visit (which represents the efficiency). Now the reason that a technician was sent to the customer site was because the technical service center could not solve the problem over the phone. So the next part of the formula deals with the percentage of calls to the technical service center that could not be solved and this is a measure of the technical service center efficiency or inefficiency as the case may be. Similarly, the technical service center would not have received the call if the customer service center solved the problem in the first place. So, another cost driver would be the customer service center efficiency. The customer service center is called because there are products out in the market and that is the unit call

Figure 5-2. Developing formulas to identify cost drivers for customer service for goods under warranty.

AIM & DRIVE: Measuring Secondary and Tertiary Costs					
PRIMARY COST : CUSTOMER SERVICE FOR GOODS UNDER WARRANTY					
CRITICAL COSTS	COST DRIVERS				
Field Service Labor	$\dfrac{\$}{hr}$ X *FS labor rate*	$\dfrac{\text{\# of hrs}}{\text{visit call}}$ X *FS efficiency*	$\dfrac{\text{\# of visit calls}}{\text{\# of calls to TSC}}$ X *TSC efficiency*	$\dfrac{\text{\# of calls to TSC}}{\text{\# of calls to CS}}$ X *CS efficiency*	$\dfrac{\text{\# of calls to CS}}{\text{units sold}}$ X *Unit call rate* $\quad\dfrac{\text{units sold}}{\text{year}}$ *Revenue driver*
Direct Material	$\dfrac{\$}{part}$ X *Unit price*	$\dfrac{\text{\# of parts}}{\text{repair}}$ X *New part requirement*	$\dfrac{\text{\# of repairs}}{\text{\# of good repairs}}$ X *Repair effectiveness*	$\dfrac{\text{\# of good repairs}}{\text{units sold}}$ X *Defect rate*	$\dfrac{\text{units sold}}{\text{year}}$ *Revenue driver*
Freight	$\dfrac{\$}{kg}$ X *Freight rate*	$\dfrac{\text{\# of kgs}}{part}$ X *Part weight*	$\dfrac{\text{\# of parts}}{\text{shipment}}$ X *Shipment size*	$\dfrac{\text{\# of shipments}}{\text{year}}$ *Shipment frequency*	

Note:
TSC = Technical Service Center
CS = Customer Service
FS = Field Service

rate. Finally, it is products that are sold that generate revenue and hence we stop at the revenue driver. When looking at some of the variables in the formula it sometimes appears that the numerator and denominator are reversed. Don't worry about that. What you are try-ing to do is maintain the logic that the numerator of the next variable is the same as the denominator of the previous variable. In the end it is the *ratio* or relationship between the numerator and denominator that matters. Similarly, the naming of a variable is totally up to the team. Using the words, TSC efficiency or TSC inefficiency still gives you a casual relationship between the cost driver and the cost element being measured.

Having written a formula for each of the secondary or tertiary costs, the elements on the RHS (cost drivers) can now be listed in column 'M' of the Master Worksheet (Figure 5-3).

It takes practice to write a good formula but once you get used to the logic you will find it extremely easy to construct formulas for just about any cost element. Take a look at the formulas developed by the Printed Manuals team in Figure 5-4. Think about the logic used by those teams. Maybe the team would like to add something or shorten another part of the formula. That is perfectly acceptable. Teams should take a first stab at a formula, look at it closely, see if it supports the process flow of activities, and then modify the formula if needed.

At first glance you might think that the only drivers would be the price of paper price and the quantity purchased. However, when stretching the formula a team can bring out drivers like the paper weight, the level of detail covered by the manual, the number of topics covered, and even the organization of the manual. I am sure you will agree that it is easier to trim 20 percent off the content of written material than it is to negotiate a further 20 percent off the price of paper, especially if you are a small player. Substitute paper for printed circuit boards or plastic or metal casings or any other basic raw material and you will see the value of stretching the formula.

The Corrugated Boxes team wrote a terrific set of formulas for inner board, pallets, and warehouse rent. The one for inner board is a classic case of the value of stretching the formula as much as possible. This looks at the whole supply chain all the way from buying the raw liner up to shipping out Zigmos (see Figure 5-5).

Case Studies

Because writing good formulas is so critical to the success of an AIM & DRIVE exercise, it will help to go outside the examples of the three teams at Anything Inc. and take a look at two case studies below,

Figure 5-3. *Master worksheet for customer service for goods under warranty.*

AIM & DRIVE: Master Worksheet

A PRIMARY COST : CUSTOMER SERVICE FOR GOODS UNDER WARRANTY   Total Spend = $23,206,000

CRITICAL COSTS	COST DRIVERS	KEY COST DRIVERS	SELECTED STRATEGY STATEMENT	ACTION ITEMS	WHO	DUE DATE
I	**M**	**D**	**R**	**I**	**VE**	**VE**
Field service labor (82%)	FS labor rate					
	FS efficiency					
	TSC efficiency					
	CS efficiency					
	Unit call rate					
Direct material (3%)	Unit price					
	New part requirement					
	Repair effectiveness					
	Defect rate					
Freight (1%)	Freight rate					
	Part weight					
	Shipment size					

Figure 5-4. Developing formulas to identify cost drivers for printed manuals.

AIM & DRIVE: Measuring Secondary and Tertiary Costs							
PRIMARY COST : PRINTED MANUALS							
CRITICAL COSTS	COST DRIVERS						
Design labor	$\dfrac{\$}{hr}$ Design labor rate	$\times \dfrac{\text{\# hrs}}{page}$ Design efficiency	$\times \dfrac{\text{\# pages}}{topic}$ Level of detail	$\times \dfrac{\text{\# topics}}{manual}$ Topics covered	$\times \dfrac{\text{\# manuals}}{set}$ Content organization	$\times \dfrac{\text{\# sets}}{Zigmo}$ Doc requirement	$\times \dfrac{\text{\# Zigmos}}{year}$ Revenue driver
Direct materials (paper)	$\dfrac{\$}{lb}$ Paper price	$\times \dfrac{\text{\# lbs}}{page}$ Paper weight	$\times \dfrac{\text{\# pages}}{topic}$ Level of detail	$\times \dfrac{\text{\# topics}}{manual}$ Topics covered	$\times \dfrac{\text{\# manuals}}{set}$ Content organization	$\times \dfrac{\text{\# sets}}{Zigmo}$ Doc requirement	$\times \dfrac{\text{\# Zigmos}}{year}$ Revenue driver
Printing	$\dfrac{\$}{\text{page printed}}$ Print price	$\times \dfrac{\text{\# pages}}{topic}$ Level of detail	$\times \dfrac{\text{\# topics}}{manual}$ Topics covered	$\times \dfrac{\text{\# manuals}}{set}$ Content organization	$\times \dfrac{\text{\# sets}}{Zigmo}$ Doc requirement	$\times \dfrac{\text{\# Zigmos}}{year}$ Revenue driver	
Translation	$\dfrac{\$}{\text{page translated}}$ Translation price	$\times \dfrac{\text{\# pages}}{topic}$ Level of detail	$\times \dfrac{\text{\# topics}}{manual}$ Topics covered	$\times \dfrac{\text{\# manuals}}{set}$ Content organization	$\times \dfrac{\text{\# sets}}{Zigmo}$ Doc requirement	$\times \dfrac{\text{\# Zigmos}}{year}$ Revenue driver	

involving temporary labor for software development and cable assembly for the battery charger that is part of a handset kit. You should see a fairly common pattern developing.

Case 1

A large financial services company engaged a provider of temporary services to supply them with a team of software programmers for a major IT project. The billing rate of $75 per hour was considered competitive for the level of skill and the region in which the work was being performed. The team broke down

AIM & DRIVE: Measuring Secondary and Tertiary Costs

PRIMARY COST : CORRUGATED BOXES

COST DRIVERS

CRITICAL COSTS: Board

Numerator	Denominator	Cost driver
$	ton	*Price of liner*
# total tons	# MSF boards	*MSF board weight*
# MSF boards	# good MSF boards	*MSF board yield*
# good MSF boards	# sheets	*Board size*
# sheets	# useable corr sheets	*Corrugated sheet yield*
# useable corr sheets	# useable flexo sheets	*Flexo sheet yield*
# useable flexo sheets	# boxes	*Box print yield*
# boxes	# good boxes produced	*Box handling yield*
# good boxes produced	# good boxes shipped	*Obsolescence*
# good boxes shipped	# good boxes received	*Shipping damage*
# good boxes received	# good boxes accepted	*Acceptance rate*
# good boxes accepted	# good boxes shipped to customer	*Anything Inc. handling yield /obsolescence*
# good boxes shipped to customer	# of Zigmos sold	*Packaging efficiency*
# of Zigmos sold	# of Zigmos	
# of Zigmos	year	*Revenue*

CRITICAL COSTS: Pallets

Numerator	Denominator	Cost driver
$	board ft	*Price*
# board ft	pallet purchased	*Size*
# pallets purchased	# pallets used	*Reusability*
# pallets used	# good pallets	*Pallets yield*
# good pallets	layer	*Stacking efficiency*
# layers	# boxes	*Layer utilization*
# boxes	pallet	*Pallet utilization*
# pallets	shipment	*Shipment size*
# shipments	year	

CRITICAL COSTS: Rent

Numerator	Denominator	Cost driver
$	sq ft	*Rate*
# sft	# usable sq ft	*Warehouse utilization*
# usable sq ft	pallet	*Pallet size*
# pallets	stack	*Height*
# stacks	# boxes stored	*Footprint utilization*
# boxes stored	# boxes purchased	*Inventory mgt efficiency*
# boxes purchased	year	

the cost of the project and determined that the base salary of the programmers, representing 50 percent of the total billing, was by far the critical cost. I remember the team leader saying that there was nothing they could reduce since the hourly rate was fairly competitive and they did not want to lose good programmers by cutting the rate. I asked them to write a formula. Initially it was pretty easy.

$$\frac{\$}{year} = \frac{\$}{hour} \times \frac{\#\ hours}{programmer} \times \frac{\#\ programmers}{year}$$

Upon further discussion and stretching the formula to reflect the process flow, this is what they listed for base salary:

Base salary	$\dfrac{\$}{hour}$ ✕	$\dfrac{\#\ hours\ paid}{\#\ hours\ worked}$ ✕	$\dfrac{\#\ hours\ worked}{\#\ of\ lines\ of\ code\ written}$ ✕	$\dfrac{\#\ of\ lines\ of\ code\ written}{\#\ of\ good\ lines\ of\ code\ written}$ ✕	$\dfrac{\#\ of\ good\ lines\ of\ code\ written}{\#\ of\ good\ lines\ of\ code\ used}$ ✕	$\dfrac{\#\ of\ good\ lines\ of\ code\ used}{feature}$ ✕	$\dfrac{\#\ of\ features}{software\ package}$ ✕	$\dfrac{\#\ of\ software\ packages}{\#\ of\ platforms}$ ✕	$\dfrac{\#\ of\ platforms}{years}$
	Wage rate	Labor utilization	Programming speed	Programming efficiency	Compliance to requirement efficiency	Feature complexity	Software complexity	Software reusability	Product release

Clearly the wage rate is one of the first cost drivers that comes to mind. However, upon probing the "ten-meter managers" they listed cost drivers like labor utilization, programming speed, programming efficiency, compliance to requirement, feature complexity, software reusability, and the number of product releases. Impressive, isn't it? Now, suddenly, the focus shifts from cutting the hourly rate to examining whether the method of writing code encouraged the programmer to think about how that code could be reused on other financial software packages. We also learned that, often, programmers will write thousands of lines of good code, only to see the client change its mind and remove a certain function or feature and add something else. So, all the time and money spent on writing good code is wasted.

Case 2

I was making an initial presentation on AIM & DRIVE to a group of senior executives and commodity leaders of a large handset manufacturer. I decided to go out on a limb and do a real live formula for them. One of the attendees took out a battery charger and handed it to me. "I am responsible for the cable assembly in this charger," he said. "What can you tell me that I don't already know about reducing the cost of this assembly?" I asked him to help me identify a key cost element and he promptly replied: "The material cost is two thirds of the price." Upon probing further he conceded that the cable and connector were the main items in the bill of material so we decided to choose the cable cost as our target for writing a formula. Again, at first glance it looked as though the formula would be a pretty short one like:

$$\frac{\$}{\text{cable}} \times \frac{\#\text{cables}}{\text{year}}$$

I was quickly reminded that neither variable had any room for improvement since the company had leveraged the best price in the market for that cable and they certainly could not reduce the volume of cables purchased. We decided to draw a rough process map and then constructed the following formula, which opened up a number of other drivers of the total cable cost per year:

Cable cost per year	$\dfrac{\$}{\text{meter}}$	$\times$	$\dfrac{\#\text{ meters}}{\text{roll}}$	$\times$	$\dfrac{\#\text{ rolls}}{\#\text{ of cut pieces}}$	$\times$	$\dfrac{\#\text{ of cut pieces}}{\#\text{ of good cut pieces}}$	$\times$	$\dfrac{\#\text{ of good cut pieces}}{\text{assembly}}$	$\times$	$\dfrac{\#\text{ of assemblies}}{\#\text{ of good assemblies}}$	$\times$	$\dfrac{\#\text{ of good assemblies}}{\text{chargers produced}}$	$\times$	$\dfrac{\#\text{ chargers produced}}{\#\text{ chargers sold}}$	$\times$	$\dfrac{\#\text{ chargers sold}}{\text{years}}$
	Cable price		Roll size		Cable length		Cutting efficiency		Assembly design		Assembly yield		Production planning efficiency		Forecast accuracy		Revenue

It may or may not have been possible to reduce the price per meter of cable purchased, but surely there were other drivers of cable cost that could be considered? The cable length perhaps? In this case, taking the cable length as a cost driver and going through the rest of the AIM & DRIVE process, a decision was taken to reduce the cable length by 30 percent. This decision did not compromise on the quality of the cable, nor the performance of the charger. It did, however, save millions of dollars and the user of the charger (the end customer) did not even notice the difference in the product.

You should now have a fairly good idea about how a list of cost drivers is constructed. Cost drivers, by definition, cause the targeted cost element to move up or down. It would be an exercise in futility to attempt to manage every one of the drivers. It would make more sense to proceed to the next step in the AIM & DRIVE, which is to define the *key* cost drivers and develop strategic options.

Checklist for Step 3: Measuring Secondary and Tertiary Costs

❏ Select the critical costs identified in Step 2.

❏ Write a formula for each of the critical costs, keeping in mind:

 • The objective is *not* to calculate numbers but to identify cost drivers.

 • In a formula the left-hand side (LHS) *must* be equal to the right-hand side (RHS).

 • The LHS represents the *cost element* being measured.

 • The RHS represents the *cost drivers.*

 • Cost drivers move within a range unless they are constants.

❏ Stretch the formula as much as possible.

❏ Name each variable (cost driver) in the equation.

❏ The end of a formula should typically be the revenue driver.

## CHAPTER 6

Defining the Key Cost Drivers and Developing Strategic Options

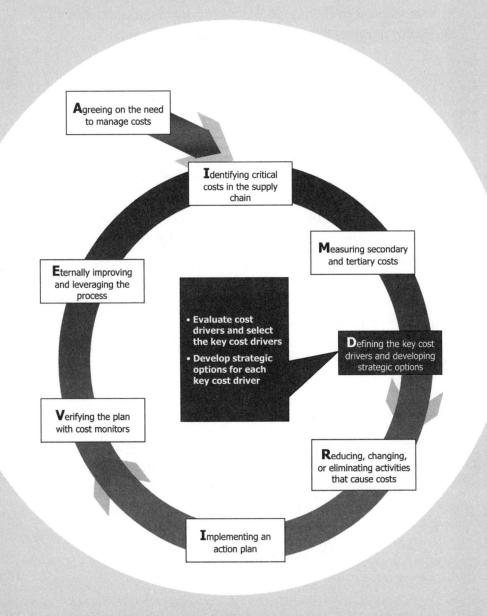

Now that you've been exposed to the logic of Formula Based Costing, you should have no difficulty recognizing a cost driver. After all, it is a variable on the right-hand side of a mathematical equation. Yet, there are times when I've asked participants in my seminars at some of the best companies in the world a question like, "Would the skill of the operators be a cost driver?" and they have replied "yes." What do you think? I'm sure you are thinking to yourself, "Of course the skill of the operator is a cost driver, since it causes a cost like scrap or direct labor." Well, try to write a formula:

$$\frac{\text{Direct}}{\text{labor}} = \frac{\$}{\text{hour}} \times \frac{\#\ \text{hours}}{\text{task}} \times \text{skill of the operator}$$

Does it make sense to you? No. Then it's time for you to settle once and for all the fact that if something is *not* listed on the right-hand side of an equation, it is *not* a cost driver, no matter what anyone says. Typically, factors like tolerances, quality of material, skill of operator, type of equipment, and so on are *functions* or *strategic options*, since they determine the current value of the variable in the equation.

The fourth step in the AIM & DRIVE process requires your team to review the list of cost drivers from your formulas in the previous step and select what you consider to be the *key cost drivers*. In other words, select the variables that, if changed, will have the biggest impact on the cost you are trying to manage.

Review the List of Current Cost Drivers

Take one more look at your formula and see if you can stretch it further. Ask yourself if it makes sense to you and the others in the team. Sometimes you may need to factor in that your formula is based on a perfect scenario. For example, if you were writing a formula for raw material such as the plastic used for making a case for your computer, the formula would read something like:

$$\frac{\$}{\text{year}} = \frac{\$}{\text{kg}} \times \frac{\text{\# kgs}}{\text{sq cm}} \times \frac{\text{\# sq cms}}{\text{sheet}} \times \frac{\text{\# sheets}}{\text{computer}} \times \frac{\text{\# computers}}{\text{year}}$$

While reviewing this you may realize that you haven't factored the yield loss. Well, you can modify your formula to either take the whole equation and divide it by yield or insert a variable like:

$$\frac{\text{\# sq cms}}{\text{sheet}} \times \frac{\text{\# sheets}}{\text{good sheet}} \times \frac{\text{\# good sheets}}{\text{computer}}$$

Here the variable, *number of sheets per good sheet*, will consider the fact that you have to buy more plastic than you need in order to make a certain number of computers. This is because you will be scrapping some of the sheets due to quality or other problems. The equation can get more complex if you can reuse some of the plastic from the sheets rejected. But I hope you get the point. Review the cost drivers and rewrite your formula if you feel that you have failed to consider a certain variable or factor that causes the left-hand side of the equation to change.

Selection of the Key Cost Driver by Observation

Once you are satisfied that your formulas are fine, list the drivers for each cost (this was done in Figure 5-2 by our Customer Services team at Anything Inc.). Now discuss the impact that each of the drivers have on a given cost or a number of cost elements. With the help of your ten-meter managers you should be able to see which one or more of the drivers would make the biggest impact. Some people feel that it is not wise to use a subjective approach to selecting key cost drivers. I would agree with them if the decision were being made by an individual without an inside knowledge of the process. However, in all probability you have a team of people that have a good knowledge of the process, key costs, and the degree of improvement possible for a given driver. Sometimes, all you have to do is use common sense. For example, in the case of our customer service costs, let's look at the total costs again in Figure 6-1. Now, look at the Master Worksheet shown again here in Figure 6-2. Observe the list of costs and cost drivers currently on the Master Worksheet. Select three drivers from the list that you think will prove to be *key* cost drivers and put it aside. Perhaps later, we'll see how close you were to the team at Anything Inc.

While making a selection by observation here are a few factors to consider:

1. If you have more than one secondary or tertiary cost, how would you distribute $100 between the respective costs? This is the same as assigning weights.
2. Which cost has the highest value?
3. What are the variables in the formula for that particular cost?
4. Are there any other variables that repeat in more than one cost element?
5. What level (high/medium/low) of impact would each variable have on the given cost element?
6. What is the current value of each variable?
7. What is the best-in-class (benchmark) value for the respective variables? Is there scope for improvement?
8. Can you and your team affect this variable?

Figure 6-1. Estimated cost of customer service for goods under warranty.

Details of Activities	Formula (if any)	Estimated Amount
1 300,000 calls to Customer Service Center—avg. 2 minutes per call @ $0.50 per minute	$(300,000 \times 2 \times \$0.50)$	$300,000
2 200,000 calls transferred to Fixit, Inc.'s Technical Service Center (TSC) @ 4 minutes per call. Service rate: $150/hour	$(200,000 \div 15 \times \$150)$	$2,000,000
3 Cost of parts needed for 1,000 calls solved by TSC @$70 each	$[1,000 \times \$(40+20+10)]$	$70,000
4 64,000 field service calls—avg. 2 hours per call @ $150/hour	$(64,000 \times 2 \times \$150)$	$19,200,000
5 Cost of parts needed for field service calls—90% of calls were solved of which 2,800 needed parts @ $70 each	$(2800 \times \$70)$	$196,000
6 Cost of defective units shipped backed to Regional Service *and* repaired. 4,480 out of 6,400 repaired at a net cost of $180 each	$[4,480 \times \$(300+20+85-225)]$	$806,400
7 Cost of defective units shipped back to RSC that were scrapped. 1,920 units were scrapped at a net cost of $330	$[1,920 \times \$(300+20+10)]$	$633,600
Total Cost of Customer Service for goods under warranty		**$23,206,000**

Figure 6-2. Master worksheet for customer service for goods under warranty.

AIM & DRIVE: Master Worksheet

A PRIMARY COST : CUSTOMER SERVICE FOR GOODS UNDER WARRANTY Total Spend = $23,206,000

CRITICAL COSTS	COST DRIVERS	KEY COST DRIVERS	SELECTED STRATEGY STATEMENT	ACTION ITEMS	WHO	DUE DATE
I	M	D	R	I	VE	VE
Field service labor (82%)	FS labor rate FS efficiency TSC efficiency CS efficiency Unit call rate					
Direct material (3%)	Unit price New part requirement Repair effectiveness Defect rate					
Freight (1%)	Freight rate Part weight Shipment size					

Develop a Model to Select the Key Cost Drivers

If you feel uncomfortable choosing a key cost driver by observation, you can put your logic into a model and then make your selection. Figure 6-3 shows such a model. Start by listing the secondary or tertiary costs from column 'I' of your Master Worksheet (Figure 6-2). For our Customer Services team at Anything Inc., the cost elements would be direct labor, direct material, and freight. Next, estimate the weights for each of the cost elements. Remember the sum of the weights must equal 100 percent. You can use actual data or, from a sample population, take actual readings and then estimate the weights. Using a combination of actual data and estimates, the Customer Services team at Anything Inc. gave direct labor a weight of 90 percent, to direct material a weight of 7 percent, and to freight, 3 percent (Figure 6-3).

Once you have assigned weights to the selected secondary/tertiary costs, list all the cost drivers (variables in the formulas) from column 'M' of your Master Worksheet in Figure 6-2. In the story of the Customer Services team at Anything Inc., the drivers would be:

- Number of calls to the customer service center (CSC)
- Percentage of those calls transferred to the technical service center (TSC)
- Number of hours per TSC call
- Hourly wage rate
- Percentage of TSC calls that required a field visit . . . and so on

If there are drivers that appear in more than one formula, list that driver only once. Now, estimate the current value (level) of the driver. This will not be so easy since accounting systems may not provide all the relevant data. Once again, you could run a sample and take actual readings. At Anything Inc., fortunately there was sufficient data to help the team. For example, there were 300,000 calls to the CSC, of which

Figure 6-3. Defining key cost drivers for customer service for goods under warranty.

AIM & DRIVE: Measuring Secondary and Tertiary Costs

PRIMARY COST : CUSTOMER SERVICE FOR GOODS UNDER WARRANTY

(D) Defining key cost drivers

Cost Drivers	Cost Elements			Score ∏(I x RP)	Current level	Amount of improvement possible H/M/L	Can we affect?	Select?
	Key : 5 = high 1 = low 3 = med 0 = no impact							
	Labor (field service techs)	Direct material (parts)	Freight					
	Relative Percentage (RP) (total = 100%)							
	95	4	1					
Labor rate ($ / hr)	5	0	0	4.75	150	L		
FS efficiency (# hrs / visit call)	3	0	0	2.85	2	H	Y	Y
TSC efficiency (# visit calls / # TSC calls)	5	0	0	4.75	32	H	Y	Y
CS efficiency (# TSC calls / # CS calls)	3	0	0	2.85	67	H	Y	Y
Unit call rate (# calls to CS / unit)	1	0	0	0.95	300,000	M		
Unit price ($ / part)	0	5	0	0.2	20	L		
New part required (# parts / repair)	0	5	0	0.04	2	L		
Repair effectiveness (# repairs / # good repairs)	0	1	0	0.12	1.05	L		
Defect rate (# good repairs / unit sold)	0	3	0	0.12	4480	M		
Freight rate ($ / kg)	0	0	5	0.05	6.25	L		
Part weight (# kgs / part)	0	0	5	0.05	0.8	L		
Shipment size (# parts / shipment)	0	0	5	0.05	2	L		
Shipment frequency (# shipments / year)	0	0	5	0.05	25,000	L		

67 percent were transferred to the TSC. From there, 32 percent resulted in a field visit. The average time per call at the TSC was 4 minutes and the average hourly rate is $150.

Having set up the list of costs and cost drivers in a matrix form you will need to discuss the impact of each driver on every cost element. You may use 5 if you believe that the driver has a high impact on a cost element, 3 if the impact is medium, 1 if it is a low impact, and 0 if the driver does not impact that cost. A rule of thumb that emanates from basic algebra is that if a driver is in the formula for a particular cost it *must* have a value greater than 0. Similarly, if a driver is *not* in the formula for a cost element it *cannot* have a value other than 0. Discussing the level of impact for each driver against each cost can be a tedious task. You will need to refer to your process map and consider the ten-meter manager's input. While it is ideal to come to a consensus, be practical and don't get carried away arguing on the merits of using an impact factor of '1' versus '3' for a cost that is 3 percent of your total cost.

Weighted Value of Cost Drivers

After filling in the impact values for each box in the matrix, the next step is to determine which of the cost drivers have the biggest impact on total costs. Of course, if the cost elements you have listed on the left-hand side of the model are more or less equal in value then it would be appropriate to simply add the values in each column of the matrix and select the one or ones with the highest total score. However, in most cases, including the customer service example, the cost elements are not equal. That's why we created the weights. Now, it is a matter of taking each column, multiplying the impact value by the weight of the respective cost element, and taking the sum of the weighted values. This is the weighted value of the impact of each driver. For example, in Figure 6-3, the team calculated the weighted value of the driver, "percentage of TSC calls that resulted in a field visit," as follows:

Impact on direct labor (95%) = 5   (every time a field visit is
                                                            made, an average $300 of
                                                            labor is incurred)
Impact on direct material (4%) = 0   (this variable is not in the
                                                            direct material formula)
Impact on freight (1%) = 0   (this variable is not in the
                                                            direct material formula)

The weighted value of the cost driver would thus be:

$$(5 \times 0.95) + (0 \times 0.04) + (0 \times 0.01) = 4.75$$

Potential for Improvement

Observe the values of the weighted cost drivers in Figure 6-3. It would be a good idea to start with about four or five drivers with the highest weighted values. In the Anything Inc. example, the top five drivers are:

• TSC Efficiency	4.75
• Labor Rate	4.75
• CS Efficiency	2.85
• FS Efficiency	2.85

For each driver, compare the current value of the driver with the benchmark value. Determining the benchmark value can be a tricky job. In some cases, this would be a theoretical maximum or minimum value (like 100 percent yield or 0 percent of calls requiring field visits). Usually, the best-in-class value is ascertained by competitive analysis or benchmarking the best companies in the respective industries or by shopping the world for rates on materials, labor, or productivity. A case in point is the hourly rate used by Fixit, Inc. in the story. While $150 per hour may appear unusually high, a competitive evaluation of rates charged by other service providers indicated an average of $185 per hour. Only two companies offering similar quality of service charged below $150 (they both charged $145 per hour). Hence the team considered the dollars per hour a significant driver with a LOW level of potential improvement.

The key question to ask in determining if a cost driver has potential for improvement is: "Will the technology, quality, safety, cycle time, or total cost of the product or service be jeopardized if you achieve the theoretical limit?" In determining the wage rate for a field service technician, one could argue that the "theoretical" minimum would be the minimum wage rate, plus statutory costs like payroll taxes. Realistically, in this story, there is about a $5 per hour potential improvement from $150 per hour to $145 per hour. This is a mere 3.33 percent. However, for the percentage of calls requiring a field visit, the current level of 34 percent indicates that there is great potential for improvement to less than 10 percent. The same goes for the percentage of Customer Service calls transferred to the Technical Service Center or for the number of hours per field visit. The best thing to do is discuss each item with your team and then determine if there is, in fact, potential to improve upon the driver.

Once you have selected the key cost drivers that have potential for improvement and you can influence or impact, enter those cost drivers in column "D" of your Master Worksheet as shown in Figure 6-4.

Developing Strategic Options for Selected Cost Drivers

Now that you have selected your key cost drivers, you need to ask yourself a very simple question: What determines the value of the

Figure 6-4. Master worksheet for customer service for goods under warranty.

AIM & DRIVE: Master Worksheet

A PRIMARY COST : CUSTOMER SERVICE FOR GOODS UNDER WARRANTY

Total Spend = $23,206,000

CRITICAL COSTS	COST DRIVERS	KEY COST DRIVERS	SELECTED STRATEGY STATEMENT	ACTION ITEMS	WHO	DUE DATE
I	**M**	**D**	**R**	**I**	**VE**	**VE**
Field service labor	FS labor rate **FS efficiency** **TSC efficiency** **CS efficiency** Unit call rate	FS efficiency (# of hrs / visit call) TSC efficiency (# of visit calls / # of calls to TSC)				
Direct material	Unit price New part requirement Repair effectiveness Defect rate					
Freight	Freight rate Part weight Shipment size	CS efficiency (# of calls to TSC / # of calls to CS)				

respective cost drivers? The answer/s you come up with would be your *functions* or *strategic options*. When working with cross-functional teams you will learn to appreciate the different perspectives that various team members bring to the discussion. Let me attempt to summarize the discussion that took place with the team at Anything Inc. and Fixit. We will focus on only one cost driver, namely, the percentage of Technical Service Center calls that require a field visit.

From Figure 6-3 you will observe that currently 32 percent of TSC calls result in a field visit. What determines this value? The team discussed the following functions as listed in Figure 6-5:

- *Number of Failures.* It goes without saying that if the product did not fail, there would not be any need to send a field service

Figure 6-5. Developing strategic options for key cost drivers of customer service for goods under warranty.

AIM & DRIVE: Developing Strategic Options

PRIMARY COST : CUSTOMER SERVICE FOR GOODS UNDER WARRANTY

	CRITICAL COSTS	
A	Field Service Labor	82.0%
B	Direct Material (parts)	3.0%
C	Freight	0.5%

KEY COST DRIVERS	RANK	A — # of hrs / visit call — *FS efficiency*	RANK	A — # of visit calls / # of calls to TSC — *TSC efficiency*	RANK	A — # of calls to TSC / # of calls to CS — *CS efficiency*
		Functions:		**Functions:**		**Functions:**
		skill level of field tech		# of failures		# of failures
	1	clarity of task		skill level of TSC tech	6	skill level of operator
		complexity of problem		complexity of problem		complexity of problem
		location of customer		level of customer knowledge		level of customer knowledge
	5	types of tools available		level of TSC workload		level of CS workload
	4	level of documentation	4	clarity of service manual		clarity of service manual
	2	level of customer knowledge	3	level of customer expectation		
		# of standard kits		established time limits		
		size of customer site				

technician to the customer. However, it would be fair to say that of the million or so Zigmos sold in the first year, only 1,920 were irreparable. Also, there is a quality assurance department constantly working on the failure rate and so the team decided to proceed with the examination of other options.

- *Skill Level of the TSC Technician.* There are two types of skills that are needed for a TSC technician to solve a customer problem over the phone, thereby avoiding a field visit. First, the technician would be expected to possess the necessary technical background and experience in order to assess the situation and determine a solution. Most Fixit engineers did, in fact, possess the required technical skills. However, as it was pointed out in the meeting, they lacked communication skills. It is no point having a solution if one is not able to communicate that solution over the phone to a customer who, probably, is not technically oriented. According to one of the TSC technicians at the meeting, certain customers were so "dumb" they could not follow the simplest of instructions, thereby forcing the technician to send a field rep to the customer's site. We had to remind the technician that the customer did not have to be a technical wiz in order to own a Zigmo and that it was the technician who needed to speak in laypeople terms.

- *Complexity of the Problem.* In many cases the problem was so complex that either the customer was unable to describe the situation to the technician, or the technician was not in a position to solve the problem over the phone. In such cases a field visit was warranted in order to study the problem at the customer site.

- *Level of Customer Knowledge.* The customer base of Anything Inc. was extremely diverse. In some cases users were technical people themselves and tended to open the product on their own and do a bit of firefighting themselves. In other cases, users were intimidated by the complexity of the Zigmo and would not venture to even open up the screws on the back. Clearly, the latter needed a lot more hand-holding and, in most cases, a field visit.

- *Level of TSC Personnel Workload.* This turned out to be a very "political" issue. According to one of the TSC supervisors, a renowned management consultant had recently concluded a reengineering project. One of the recommendations was that the TSC could be downsized by 20 percent. The typical advice to the supervisor was, "Make sure your people work smarter." According to this high-priced consulting firm, the average call should be completed in four minutes versus the previous average of five minutes. To ensure that technicians were conscious of time, the consultant proposed that new telephones be provided to the TSC. These phones would show the time per call, signal the technician when he/she had one minute more, and, with the most irritating of messages, recommend that the technician take down the customer's information and send out a field rep. I remember the supervisor getting red in the face with anger as he described this to the rest of the team. "In some cases, my technicians get so frustrated that they shout 'shut up' over the phone. It takes more than four minutes to explain to the shocked customer that you were not talking to them." A TSC engineer piped in that, many a time, they could have solved the problem in a few more minutes, but had to follow the instructions of management and terminate the call, sending a $150-an-hour engineer out to the customer. Believe me, the group had some choice words for both the consultant and their management.

- *Clarity of the Service Manual.* Have you ever had a product with a very complex service manual? Well, sad to say, the Zigmo was one of those products. A quick poll of a few non-technical users of the Zigmo indicated that fewer than 15 percent of the people had ever bothered to read their service manual. It had been written by engineers, for engineers. The average user found it too complex, badly organized, and certainly not user-friendly. Needless to say, once word got out that the manuals were not helpful to the average user; many new users didn't even bother to remove the shrinkwrap. Sounds familiar? To them it was far easier to call a toll-free number and request that a field technician go over immediately to solve the problem. Typically, they were not interested in describing the problem over the phone, much less listening to a technician provide a solution, which they had to implement on their own.

- *Level of Customer Expectation.* During the preceding discussion it was apparent that the focus of the team was on reducing cost. Somehow, the marketing representative pointed out, the team had failed to realize that customer service was designed to satisfy the needs of the customer. She went on to observe that there were a few customers who felt slighted when they were required to deal with a technical representative over the phone. Perhaps there was a perception that unless a field representative came to solve a problem at the customer's site, the service level was considered to be inadequate. I remember the marketing representative saying to the group at Anything Inc., "Even though sending a field representative costs more money, I'm willing to spring for it from my budget in the case of certain key customers. What's a few thousand bucks compared to the cost of losing a contract worth millions of dollars?" The rest of the team agreed that, like it or not, certain customers expected to see a person when they had a problem and not have to go through the process of explaining the problem over the phone to a technical rep.

The two other teams at Anything Inc. decided to define the key cost drivers by observation, which was fine since they had the right people on the team and went through the logic for selecting the key drivers. You would imagine that with 84 percent of the cost of printed manuals being the paper cost, the team would have chosen the price of paper as its top cost driver (see Figure 6-6). Not so. That does not mean they did not want to work on the price of paper. It is just that they realized that the level of detail, which determined the total number of printed pages in the manual, had far greater impact on material, design labor, printing, and translation costs than any other driver in their list.

Having ranked the level of detail, the number of documents printed (document requirements), and the paper price as their three key cost drivers, note how the team listed a bunch of strategic options

Figure 6-6. List of key cost drivers by observation for printed manuals.

AIM & DRIVE: Defining Key Cost Drivers

PRIMARY COST : PRINTED MANUALS

CRITICAL COSTS	RANK	Design labor	RANK	Direct materials (paper)	RANK	Printing	RANK	Translation
% of Total Supplier Cost		4%		84%		10%		2%
COST DRIVERS	1	Design labor rate Design efficiency Level of detail Topics covered Content org.	3 1	Paper price Paper weight Level of detail Topics covered Content org.	1	Print price Level of detail Topics covered Content org.	1	Translation price Level of detail Topics covered Content org.
	2	Doc requirement Revenue driver	2	Doc requirement Revenue driver	2	Doc requirement Revenue driver	2	Doc requirement Revenue driver

Figure 6-7. List of strategic options for key cost drivers of printed manuals.

AIM & DRIVE: Developing Strategic Options			

PRIMARY COST : PRINTED MANUALS

	CRITICAL COSTS	
A	Design Labor	4%
B	Direct Materials (Paper)	84%
C	Printing	10%
D	Translation	2%
	Total	100%

KEY COST DRIVERS	RANK	A, B, C, D (100%)	RANK	A, B, C, D (100%)	RANK	B (84%)
		# pages		# sets		$
		topic		Zigmo		lb
		level of detail		*doc requirement*		*paper price*
		amount of information		customer requirements	4	grade of paper
		page layout (size, margins, font)		# Zigmos purchased by customer		market forces
		# of graphics	3	# customers with multiple Zigmos		# of suppliers
	2	% of information on other media				location of suppliers
	1	# of features preloaded				volume of purchase
		language used				stability of volume
						supplier's sourcing capabilities

for each of those drivers in Figure 6-7. Again, this is the idea bank so look closely at what they wrote for their list of options or functions for the price of paper: grade of paper, market forces, number of suppliers, location of suppliers, volume of purchase, stability of volume, supplier's sourcing efficiency, and supplier capabilities. The cost driver could have been the price of any other commodity and these same options would be relevant. That is the beauty of putting ideas down in writing. Other teams can leverage from those. The list can only get better but not worse.

The Corrugated Boxes team listed all their cost drivers against the respective cost elements as seen in Figure 6-8. They selected the three key cost drivers by observation: the price for liner, pallet utilization, and the level of obsolescence. Like the other two teams, this team also developed an exhaustive list of functions or options for each of the three drivers, listed in Figure 6-9. They later ranked the options and chose the number of pallet alternatives and the type of middle

Figure 6-8. List of key cost drivers by observation for corrugated boxes.

AIM & DRIVE: Defining Key Cost Drivers						
PRIMARY COST : CORRUGATED BOXES						
% of Total Supplier Cost		37%		4%		9%
CRITICAL COSTS	RANK	Board	RANK	Pallets	RANK	Rent
COST DRIVERS	1	Liner price Mix MSF board weight MSF board yield Board size Corrugated sheet yield Flexo sheet yield Box print yield Box handling yield		Pallet price Size Reusability Pallets yield Stacking efficiency Layer utilization		Lease rate Warehouse utilization Pallet size Height Footprint utilization Inventory mgt. efficiency
	3	Obsolescence Shipping damage Supplier acceptance rate Supplier handling yield Final shipping damage Anything Inc. acceptance rate handling yield obsolescence Packaging efficiency	2	Pallet utilization Shipment size		

liner board as the two strategic options on which they intended to perform a risk-benefit analysis.

With a list of key cost drivers and strategic options for each of those drivers, you are in a position to move on to the next step of the AIM & DRIVE process, which is to reduce, change, or eliminate those activities that cause costs.

Supply Chain Cost Management

Figure 6-9. List of strategic options for key cost drivers of corrugated boxes.

AIM & DRIVE: Developing Strategic Options

PRIMARY COST : CORRUGATED BOXES

		CRITICAL COSTS	
	A	Inner	
	B	Medium C	
	C	Middle liner	37.0%
	D	Medium E	
	E	Outer	
	F	Pallets	4.0%
	G	Rent	9.0%

KEY COST DRIVERS		B, D		A, B, C, D, E		F
	RANK	$ / ton	RANK	# good boxes produced / # good boxes shipped Mark	RANK	# boxes / pallet
		Liner price		*Obsolescence*		*Pallet utilization*
		Functions:		Functions:		Functions:
		market conditions		forecast accuracy		material
		chip prices		EOL/efficiency of planning process		truck height
		old corru container prices		overruns		size of box
		energy costs		quantity per run		pallet size
		geographic location		level of communication	1	# of pallet alternatives
		time of year		product lifecycle		type of flute
		# of suppliers		stability of market		
	2	type of middle liner		product design changes		
		type of flute		product acceptance		
		volume-leverage				
		volume commitment				
		lead time				

Checklist for Step 4: Defining Key Cost Drivers and Developing Strategic Options

❑ List the cost elements that you identified as critical cost elements in Step 2.

❑ List the cost drivers for each of those cost elements based on your formula.

❑ Eliminate repetitive names of cost drivers.

❑ Assign weights to each cost element based on their respective values.
Evaluate the impact of each cost driver on its corresponding cost element.

❑ Calculate the weighted impact score of each cost driver.

❑ Determine the current value of the cost drivers listed.

❑ Determine the potential in the value of each cost driver.

❑ Determine whether the team can impact the value of each cost driver.

❑ Select three or four key cost drivers based on your calculations (matrix) or by observation.

❑ For each selected cost driver list as many factors that affect the value of that driver.

❑ Rank the factors in order of importance for strategy development.

❑ Select four or five factors or strategic options to carry over to the next step.

❑ Update the Master Worksheet.

Reducing, Eliminating, or Changing Activities That Cause Costs

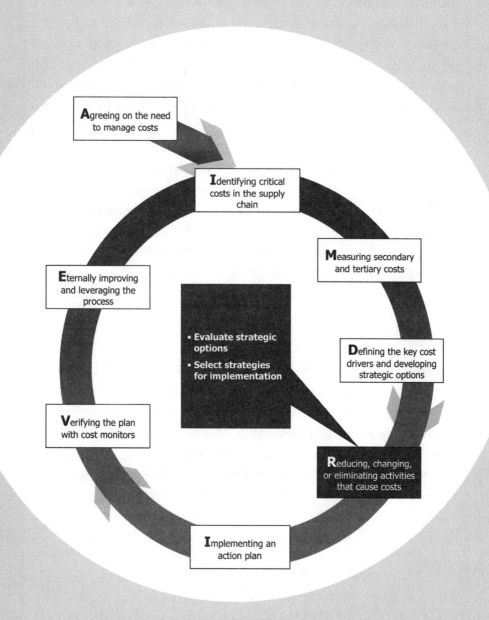

While working with numerous teams from a wide range of industries, I've come to the conclusion that writing a strategy is viewed as a theoretical exercise by many a cost management team. For some reason known only to them, these teams believe that discussing a few alternatives and choosing one or more will result in costs leaving the supply chain. Why bother writing a strategy? Good question. The objective of the fifth step in the AIM & DRIVE process is to discipline a team to think through the strategic options listed in the previous step (defining the key cost drivers and developing strategic options), to formulate enactable options, to discuss various constraints, risks, and benefits, and then to select and prioritize the options that would result in the best solution for the supply chain. Another good reason to write a strategy is that not everyone is going to be at the same job for years and years. Ideas need to be captured and used by others who follow. Before considering strategic options and performing a risk-benefit analysis, it is worth taking a look at some general strategies that work better in given situations depending on the balancing of risk and the expected return from that strategy. A typical risk return model is discussed in the following paragraphs.

The Risk-Return Model

Strategic options tell us "how" a cost driver could be reduced, changed, or eliminated in order to impact a given cost element. Sometimes it may not be possible to use a certain strategic option because of a given situation or relationship between the customer and supplier. Take a closer look at the quadrants in Figure 7-1. Each quadrant represents a type of relationship that may exist in a given situation.

Let's walk through each of these quadrants for a closer look.

Figure 7-1. Risk-return model for choosing appropriate strategic options.

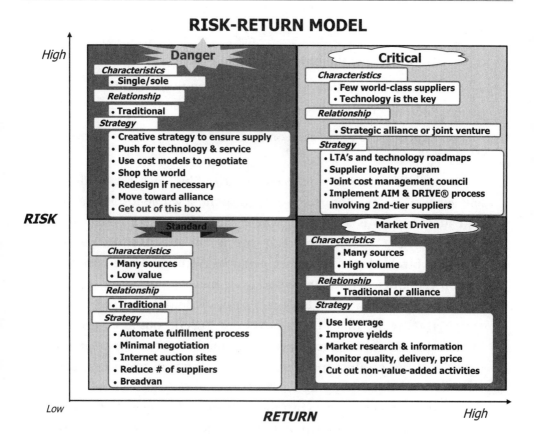

RISK-RETURN MODEL

Danger

Characteristics
- Single/sole

Relationship
- Traditional

Strategy
- Creative strategy to ensure supply
- Push for technology & service
- Use cost models to negotiate
- Shop the world
- Redesign if necessary
- Move toward alliance
- Get out of this box

Critical

Characteristics
- Few world-class suppliers
- Technology is the key

Relationship
- Strategic alliance or joint venture

Strategy
- LTA's and technology roadmaps
- Supplier loyalty program
- Joint cost management council
- Implement AIM & DRIVE® process involving 2nd-tier suppliers

Standard

Characteristics
- Many sources
- Low value

Relationship
- Traditional

Strategy
- Automate fulfillment process
- Minimal negotiation
- Internet auction sites
- Reduce # of suppliers
- Breadvan

Market Driven

Characteristics
- Many sources
- High volume

Relationship
- Traditional or alliance

Strategy
- Use leverage
- Improve yields
- Market research & information
- Monitor quality, delivery, price
- Cut out non-value-added activities

RISK — High / Low

RETURN — Low / High

Standard

The bottom left quadrant is considered the "low return–low risk" or "standard" area. Typically, this situation is characterized by many sources of low-value products or services. The relationship between customer and supplier is usually traditional, not because a partnership would not work, but because it is not considered top priority in strategy building. Strategic options that work well in the standard area are:

- Automating of the order fulfillment process
- Minimizing the time and effort spent on negotiation
- Reducing the number of suppliers
- Applying the bread van concept

Since the "standard" area is characterized by low-value products and services, it does not make sense to spend a whole lot of time on bureaucracy. This is a situation where the procurement card works well. Or, where a corporate credit card is not available, it's best to allow the buyer to use his or her personal credit card and have the person reimbursed through a weekly or bi-weekly expense report. You would think that most large companies would do this, wouldn't you? Yet, there are times that a buyer has to send out a request for quotation, receive the quote, process a purchase order, arrange for delivery of the product, process an invoice (sent in triplicate), and issue a check for a whopping $9.95 in order to purchase a book.

There are times when a customer gets carried away with the need to "negotiate" every transaction to death. I don't know what purpose is achieved by driving another $50 off a $5,000 transaction, which probably takes four or five hours of your time. Wouldn't it be better to spend the same amount of time on something more significant? Sometimes it's wiser to let a few small fires burn, let those few extra dollars go, and focus on areas where more significant costs can be taken out of the supply chain.

Another strategy that works well in the standard area is the reduction in the number of suppliers. Paring down the supply base does not mean getting into a single source situation. Often, for maintenance, repair, and operations (MRO) items, small service contracts, and shop supplies, it makes a lot more sense to deal with a select few suppliers with a sufficient amount of competition so that the select few who stay do not get too complacent.

Perhaps the strategy that works best in the standard area is the "bread van." This method is based on a system used to deliver bread in small towns or communities a couple of decades ago. The baker would load his or her van with fresh bread and drive around a neighborhood personally delivering the required amount of bread to local families. Typically, houses were not locked and the baker would enter a household, check the bread bin to verify the existing stock of bread, and leave a certain number of loaves of bread. If a member of the family happened to be present, the baker would stop to chat (or gossip as the case may be). He or she would be the first to know if relatives or friends were about to visit (which meant that more bread was needed). At the end of the month the customer was invoiced and, in many cases, money would be left on the kitchen counter for the baker to collect the next day. No one argued about the accuracy of the invoice and there did not seem to be a shortage of bread. There was really no need to do so. First, because it was an established relationship, and second, the amount involved was so small that it was not worth ruining one's reputation for the sake of a few bucks.

Today many companies use the bread van concept to stock their spare parts, office supplies, and other MRO items. DuPont and Ford successfully implemented the bread van concept on paint used on certain Ford models. DuPont was given the responsibility to provide the required amount of paint, of a specific color, for certain models of cars that came off the Ford production line. Using a system of electronic data interchange (EDI), DuPont was aware of the production schedule at Ford and the exact colors required for the day's production. It was up to DuPont to have the right amount of paint, in the right color, at the right time. The amount of paint required to paint a car was established and the price per gallon of paint negotiated as part of a long-term contract. There was one purchase order and no invoices. At the end of each month, Ford would electronically transfer a fixed sum (more like a retainer) to DuPont. At the end of the year, when the exact number of cars painted was known, a final settlement was made through one transfer of funds from Ford to DuPont—or the other way if DuPont had been overpaid. Considering the size of these companies and the high overheads involved, this procedure saved both companies hundreds of thousands of dollars.

Market-Driven

The bottom right-hand side of the model is characterized by high volume and many sources. This area represents a high return for relatively low risk. Typical strategies for a market-driven commodity include:

- Using leverage to maximize buying power
- Working with suppliers to maximize yields
- Conducting market research and gathering information to take advantage of opportunities in a given market
- Monitoring quality, delivery, and price
- Cutting out non-value-added activities

In a market-driven environment companies have succeeded in obtaining discounts from suppliers in exchange for higher volumes. This means reducing the number of suppliers and placing more business with the selected ones. However, the benefits of leverage are not restricted to large companies with high volumes. Sometimes one has to be innovative. An appliance maker that bought high volumes of sheet metal products but few electronic components found that it could leverage off the volumes of a computer company that bought high volumes of electronic components and relatively low volumes of sheet metal parts. The computer company through its international procurement offices in Asia purchased power supplies, PC boards, and display panels on behalf of the appliance maker using its leverage with those suppliers. In turn, the appliance maker was able to increase its leverage with sheet metal suppliers in eastern Europe by purchasing on behalf of itself as well as the computer company. Since these were not competing companies, it was indeed a win-win situation for all. In other cases, smaller noncompeting companies have formed consortiums in order to leverage common parts or services in a market-driven environment.

Besides using leverage to lower the purchase price of market-driven products or services, customer-supplier relationships can be elevated to the level of partners or strategic alliances where there is a common focus of improving yields at the customer's site. In other words, let's say the price of a widget is $2.00, the volume of finished product required is 10,000,000 units, and the current yields are around 90 percent. This means a customer company would have to buy 11,111,111 units and spend $22,222,222 in order to manufacture 10,000,000 good ones. It makes the purchase price of a good unit $2.22. What if, through a joint effort, the yield is increased to 95 percent? The customer would now have to buy 10,526,316 units in order to make 10,000,000 good ones. The total price paid would be $21,052,632 or an average of $2.105 per part. This is common sense, but I cannot tell you how many times I've seen customers throw in the towel and resign themselves to the fact that they are small players in the market and thus have no way to reduce the cost of a market-driven commodity.

You may not be in a position to control your market, but surely you could increase your knowledge of the marketplace? By studying the dynamics of market forces that impact your commodity or service, you will be able to take action that gives your company a competitive advantage during a sudden change in market conditions. A computer company I work closely with carefully tracked the disk drive market by following, among other trends, the value of closing inventories. Having noticed the value of inventories shooting up over a given period, it decided to look at some of its key disk drive suppliers' financial statements. Observing that one key supplier had built up a rather high inventory of finished goods, the computer company negotiated to buy a significant portion of the inventory at 30 cents on the dollar. The reason for the increase in inventory apparently was due to the introduction of a new model disk drive. However, the computer company, noted for its ability to service customers of earlier models, needed the old drives to support models of the computer that used the old drive. No one expects you to predict the future with a crystal ball. If you did, you wouldn't be working for the company you now work for. However, a sharp analyst is expected to know his/her market and be proactive in taking some calculated risks.

Other typical strategies in a market-driven environment include the careful monitoring of quality and delivery apart from price. Improvement in the quality of the material reduces the cost of rework or scrap, while good delivery performance reduces the need to maintain large inventories. It may not be easy to establish the exact impact of higher quality or more reliable delivery, but who can deny that it is worth money. If you believe in total cost management, this money is equal to a discount in the material price.

Danger Zone

This is the area where most customers hate to be, but find themselves in much too often. It is the top left quadrant of Figure 7-1 and is characterized by single or sole source suppliers. Single sourcing arises when, despite the presence of competition, a customer decides to work with only one supplier. A sole source exists when there is one, and only one, supplier for a given product or service. The relationship is more confrontational than it should be. Win-win often turns out to be a situation where the supplier wins . . . and wins again. It really doesn't have to be this way. Yes, I know you have been burned by a single or sole source that let you down in the past, or that has taken advantage of its strength in a particular market niche. There are two paths you could follow. One is to complain about the engineer or internal customer who got you into this mess, or throw your hands up in defeat. The second is to make the best of a situation. Obviously, we're talking about the difference between an eternal pessimist and a proactive optimist. Here are some of the proven strategies that the latter group (the proactive optimists) have used when faced with a situation described in the Danger Zone:

- Creative strategy to ensure supply.
- Push for technology and service.
- Use cost models to negotiate.
- Shop the world.
- Redesign if necessary.
- Move toward an alliance.
- Get out of this box!

When you are serious about managing the total cost of the supply chain, you cannot ignore the cost of lost sales. Yes, it is difficult to put a number on this. Besides, the number will change on you depending on your selling price, variable costs, number of alternatives available to your customer, and the loyalty of that customer. In any case, you've got to ask yourself, What is the cost to my company if this single or sole source supplier does not deliver the right amount of the product or service at the right time? Also, how is the internal customer going to feel about not getting the required quantity of the product or service when it is needed most? The solution is for you to come up with a creative strategy to ensure supply of the product or service, on time, every time.

Notice I used the term "creative" strategy. Sometimes creativity means doing something that makes common sense, but that you just don't do for some reason or the other. Here's one for starters. *Treat your single or sole source suppliers like you would your best customer.* Wow! That's an idea? At a large computer company buyers nearly fell off their seats laughing when I proposed this. Fortunately the head of Procurement (worldwide), being a visionary, decided to take the issue seriously. We asked the team leaders of key commodities to make a list of those single or sole source suppliers that had the ability to shut down a line or jeopardize a customer's order. We laid down some general guidelines on the treatment of such suppliers by the members of the procurement community. Believe it or not, the guidelines included picking the supplier representatives up from the airport and driving them to their hotel. If possible, arrange for a bowl of fruit or flowers or a bottle of wine to be delivered to the room. If the meeting was scheduled in the plant, arrange to pick them up, drive them to the plant, conduct the meeting, arrange a plant tour if possible, have a senior manager drop in to say "hello," and present them with a memento (it could be a small gift of less than $25 if you're worried about the ethical issue). If the evening is open, take your "guest" to something memorable. Perhaps a famous site or ball game or even, in the case of some overseas suppliers, to a popular mall. I've taken Japanese visitors to Costco in San Diego and they've appreciated it more than any gift you could give them. And, finally, if it's OK with your family, take them and the rest of your team to your *home* for dinner. You didn't read this wrong. I said take them home. People balk at the idea. What would the auditors say? Really, if your company is worried that a "team" from your company is going to show favor to one supplier because you had a meal in the home of one of the team members, shame on your management. Besides, you are not going to do this with every supplier. Only those who could "sink" you. Think that is a good enough reason to do something out of the box? I think so.

At Harley Davidson, supply chain leaders do not worry too much about having single or sole source suppliers. Harley believes that just like their loyal customers, suppliers too can be loyal and do whatever it takes to make Harley succeed. Supplier loyalty is not something that can be demanded. It has to be earned. And Harley has earned the trust, respect, and loyalty of their key suppliers by treating them as an extension of their business; treating them as they would those millions of loyal Harley customers.

Other creative strategies that I have seen work well include paying the supplier earlier than the normal payment terms, offering them a piece of other business opportunities at your company, and so on.

Most suppliers who land up in the Danger Zone are typically technology leaders, although some may get there due to carelessness on the part of your Purchasing Department. In the case of the former, it would help your company if you stopped lamenting the fact that you are "stuck" with a single or sole source. Instead, recognize the supplier as the market leader in technology and push them to include you in their new technology and service. I've seen many a company in the Danger Zone conduct valuable seminars and workshops for certain customers who requested it of them. These programs have helped the client company improve in the areas of quality, delivery, or manufacturing excellence. Consider the benefits of such workshops as a "cost reduction" in the product or service you buy from this single or sole source supplier. Then, you wouldn't feel so miserable.

Just because you find yourself in the Danger Zone doesn't mean you have to roll over and play dead. It pays to develop a cost model and renegotiate where you see some opportunities. In the case of a software or consulting contract, you may be locked in on a project's time and rates. However, to show that you are awake and alert, you could occasionally challenge the supplier if you find some invoices way out of line. For example, a proactive supply chain manager at a utility company I work with was concerned about the invoices presented by a leading consulting company. In most cases the consulting company had been chosen by a senior executive and all that was required of Procurement was to push through the papers. Nevertheless, this individual decided to put together a cost model based on industry statistics and the consulting company's 10-K report. He noticed that 47 percent of the revenue generated was paid out to those who actually performed the job. Well, when he received an invoice for a staggering amount at the completion of a particular phase, the proactive manager calculated the direct cost to be 47 percent of the staggering number. Estimating the time it took to perform that particular phase, he calculated that the people working on the project were charged out at $160 an hour. However, checking industry averages for the type of skill required, he found out that the going rate was $60 to $80 an hour. All he did was share his concerns and calculations with the consulting firm and they lopped off nearly 50 percent from the invoice. Needless to say, the practice was never repeated again. Yes, the consultant could have huffed and puffed and threatened to pull out. However, if your logic is sound you can stand your ground. Even if you pay the full invoice price, you've made your point and it is unlikely that you will be overcharged again.

In some cases, the customer merely *perceives* that it is in the Danger Zone. It is so easy to get complacent and throw in the towel. Keep in mind that global business has undergone a major change in the last decade. Today, nothing is impossible. If a provider of goods or services takes the customer base for granted, it is quite possible that the customer will go elsewhere in the world and if an alternative does not exist today, it will pretty soon. Even giants like Intel and Microsoft know that. The pool of talent available in India, China, and the Asia Pacific countries for the technology area and eastern Europe and Russia for precision parts should make any western "giant" think twice before mauling their customers. So, shop the world and the world is yours. Think local and you will be part of those left behind in the race.

Finally, as the saying goes, "If you can't beat 'em, join 'em." There have been cases when a customer has found itself in the Danger Zone with a critical supplier. Depending on the size of the customer and what it has to offer a single or sole source supplier, it may be possible to move toward a strategic alliance. If the customer is a technology leader it is quite possible that the single or sole source supplier would want to continue holding that position in the marketplace. But, that requires being at the leading edge of technology going forward as well. In such cases, it is not uncommon to hear of the customer and single or sole source supplier working on technology convergence, where both companies share their respective technology road maps and work toward a common technology platform. Yes, that perpetuates having a single or sole source relationship but it is a decision that is taken after careful consideration of the risks and benefits. The expectation is that a strategic alliance will give the customer the first crack at the new technology and possibly assurance of supply of that technology. This, in itself, will give the customer a competitive edge and extricate itself from the Danger Zone.

The bottom line, of course, is, Get out of this box! if you find your competitiveness is being threatened by being inside it.

Critical

This is the "nirvana" of a relationship. Needless to say, there may be only very few supplier/customer relationships that will reach this level and stay there. The top right quadrant of Figure 7-1 is characterized by the presence of only a few world-class suppliers. In this area, technology is usually the key. Or, as in the semiconductor business, the financial outlay required to enter the field is prohibitive, so new suppliers do not emerge. This is where strategic alliances and joint ventures flourish. Cost management strategies that work best here are:

- Development of long-term agreements (LTAs) and technology road maps
- Building a supplier loyalty program
- Formation of joint cost management councils
- Implementation of the AIM & DRIVE process with second-tier suppliers

It is extremely hard for a relationship to flourish and both sides to trust one another if either side is not willing to commit to a long-term relationship. Sometimes the relationship needs to be formalized in the form of a long-term agreement or contract. It's not that the two or more parties need to have a written agreement in order to have a good relationship. Quite the contrary. It is the written agreement that clearly spells out the commitment made by all parties and the expectations that each can have of the other. The result of such agreements paves the way for breakthrough ideas and really long-term strategies.

Long-Term Agreements and Technology Road Maps. When Gene Richter joined IBM as the Chief Procurement Officer, one of the first tasks he set for himself and his team was to identify critical suppliers that would bring IBM back to the forefront of technology. Within a year numerous global long-term agreements were signed with the best of the suppliers in various areas from memory cards to distribution. IBM was a tough customer, but Richter and his Technology and

Qualification Vice President, Sang Park, proved that IBM could open up and share some of its long-term goals with those suppliers. Initially, the change was difficult for many in IBM's development group. The idea of developing technology road maps and striving for technology convergence was something the old IBM would not have looked kindly upon. However, when the new IBM put together the first such forum with critical suppliers, the results were astounding. With representatives from key suppliers willing to share sensitive data and provide IBM with positive criticism about its qualification process, IBM had the "Dream Team" on its side. None of these suppliers were concerned about losing business share since they had entered into long-term agreements—and there was enough of IBM business to go around. Suppliers opened up. And Big Blue listened. Now, who would be willing to do all this for a customer if they were likely to be thrown out the next day or year if a cheaper supplier showed up at the door?

Supplier Loyalty Programs. A lot of companies talk about supplier partnerships, alliances, and cooperation. Very few, however, think about supplier loyalty as the ultimate proof of such relationships. As pointed out earlier in the chapter, Harley Davidson is one such company. At Harley, there is a management-sponsored program to build supplier loyalty within its supply base. In order to build supplier loyalty, Harley proves to the supplier that it is a loyal customer. Rarely, if at all, will Harley category teams get rid of loyal suppliers just because there was another bid that came in a few points lower. Like many Japanese companies, when a supplier has a problem, Harley considers it their problem as well and joins forces with the supplier to overcome it. Loyalty is about actions and not words. How many companies can claim that their CEO sets aside sixty days a year to visit with key suppliers? I know one that can. Harley Davidson.

Cost Management Councils. Once the terms of a long-term agreement have been ironed out, it's time to set up a joint cost management council. This council consists of a few key executives from all sides of the alliance responsible for the flow of funds through their respective parts of the supply chain. Ideally, members of the cost management council would be someone from the Financial Controller's office, Procurement, Manufacturing, and in the case of service contracts, the key user department. All written strategies should be presented to the council and critiqued by it. Follow-up meetings should be held from time to time in order to maintain the momentum. We'll discuss this in greater detail in Chapter 9.

If the strategic alliance or joint venture successfully implements AIM & DRIVE projects, it would help to spread the process to the second-tier suppliers. Texas Instruments did a good job at this in the mid-1990s. After spending two years training first-tier suppliers and implementing AIM & DRIVE projects in the United States, Japan, Philippines, Taiwan, Singapore, and Europe, it appeared that TI had scraped the bottom of the bowl of cost savings. I remember the leader of the AIM & DRIVE initiative saying, "Why don't we drill down into the second tier?" At first it appeared that this would not work since the teams at TI were already spread thin and could not take on such a major initiative. The solution came from TI Europe: a proposal to sponsor a pilot training program for those first-tier suppliers who had demonstrated a willingness to apply the AIM & DRIVE process with their own suppliers. I remember doing this class in Brussels and it was the first time I had taught the process to the suppliers' suppliers. Second-tier suppliers were taught the AIM & DRIVE process and were required to work with the key suppliers of TI in developing cost management strategies. TI, in turn, would require its suppliers to keep the Commodity Management Team (CMT) leaders posted with the results, as was the norm in the Total Quality Management process. In other words, the customer does not have to micromanage a supplier's suppliers. Rather, monitor performance by having each supplier provide the customer with the Master Worksheet of its AIM & DRIVE projects with key second-tier suppliers.

Identifying Constraints

Before launching into the creation and discussion of strategy statements, it is imperative that the team discuss whether there are any constraints that they have to deal with. A constraint is a limiting factor that must be taken into consideration before a strategic option is considered by your team. It is something that is physically or organizationally impossible to execute. Constraints must be discussed before the risk-benefit analysis of a strategic option is considered. Often, I've witnessed teams discuss a constraint, like safety for example, and talk themselves into accepting a potentially dangerous strategy because of the huge savings potential. Imagine if an engineer were bullied by management into changing a specification, such as going with a cheaper material or having a wider tolerance, that later caused the product to electrocute a customer! (And imagine the law suit, and the potential for punitive damages!) Now, this does not mean that we abandon every strategy statement in fear of "what might happen, if . . ." Constraints need to be carefully considered and the team should come to a unanimous decision about what is absolutely out of bounds. Here are some topics that generate healthy discussion on constraints:

- Technology
- Quality
- Cycle time
- Safety

- Environment

- Regulation

- Time to market

- Service level

- Cost

- Ethics

In the case of Anything Inc., marketing had promised the customer that if a problem could not be solved in forty-eight hours, the customer would be given a new or refurbished Zigmo. This promise becomes a prohibitive constraint on the option of moving the field service operation, repair center, and warehouse to a distant country, since it would be impossible to fly someone out to fix the problem at a customer site within the promised time. In another case it could be a time-to-market issue, where a company is facing a very tight deadline for the launch of a new product and there is no time to change suppliers regardless of how much money can be saved. I've seen every one of the topics listed above be a constraint in one situation and not in another. All except "ethics," where there can be no compromise. If an option violates the ethical values of a company it should be shot down, regardless of potential savings. Period. Argument closed.

Figure 7-2 is a template that can be used to list any constraints the team may put on itself after a robust discussion and considering different perspectives.

Creating Strategy Statements

In Figure 6-5 you may have noticed that the strategic options had been listed as phrases like "number of failures, skill level of technical center representative, level of customer expectation," and so on. Creating a strategy statement involves taking one of your strategic options

Figure 7-2. Constraints worksheet for customer service for goods under warranty.

AIM & DRIVE: Reducing, Changing, or Eliminating Activities	
PRIMARY COST : CUSTOMER SERVICE FOR GOODS UNDER WARRANTY	
Perspective / Origin (e.g. Finance, Technology, Marketing, etc.)	CONSTRAINTS
Marketing	Turnaround time for existing customers cannot go beyond 48 hours

and putting a verb before the statement and an explanation (how, and perhaps why) after it. Take another look at this worksheet. A couple of the strategic options that the team from Anything Inc. wanted to pursue were:

- Level of customer knowledge
- Replacement policy

What would you suggest we do about the "level of customer knowledge?" How about "increase" the level of customer knowledge? That would not be a precise statement since it does not address either how or why. So we massage the statement to read, "Increase the level of customer knowledge by creating in-house technicians for major accounts." The objective of this strategy is to reduce the number of field visits by having a more knowledgeable source at the customer's site. This would involve training a few representatives at major customers who could then provide internal support if someone needed assistance on minor problems. And if that person was not able to fix the problem, he or she would contact the technical service center of Fixit and explain the problem. The in-house technician would be much better able to articulate the problem clearly to the service technician on the phone. This gives the service technician a much better chance of resolving the issue and not having to send a field technician to the customer site.

Similarly, for the second strategic option, "replacement policy," what verb would we use? How about "change"? Once again, we've got to address the how or the why. A good strategy statement would read something like, "Change replacement policy to allow the supplier to ship new/refurbished unit to customer via two-day service and have customer send defective units directly to the repair center." Again, the objective is to reduce the number of field visits.

The important thing to remember is that a strategy statement should be precise. Many times we find teams using statements like "change the specification." From what? To what? Would you be able to understand something as vague as that? Then why make someone else have to guess what's on your mind?

Evaluate Risks and Benefits from Different Perspectives

Having completed a list of strategy statements, the next step is to conduct a thorough risk-benefit analysis. Notice, the term used is "risk-benefit" and not "cost benefit" analysis. The reason is that there is more than cost involved in a decision. Besides, a strategy to reduce, change, or eliminate something has consequences for the business and, thus, must be viewed from different perspectives. Here are some of the commonly used criteria in a good risk-benefit analysis.

Financial. Of course, it is most likely that the first part of the risk-benefit discussion on a given strategy statement will focus on the monetary aspects. It is important that the team does not become "creative" in counting savings or costs. It makes sense to validate some of the calculations or, at least, challenge the logic. Here are some tips on calculating the monetary benefits of a strategy statement:

- Multiply the savings per unit by the projected twelve-month volume.

- If the strategy can be used on other part numbers or projects, make sure to extrapolate the savings over the extended volume and note that this constitutes "leverageable savings."

- In some cases the savings may take place over a number of years. This requires special consideration since there are times when a major investment is required and if we only estimate savings over the next twelve months, it may not justify the investment or up-front costs. My recommendation is that, in such cases, you project the savings over the estimated volume over the next three years and then discount those numbers back to present value using the company's cost of capital as the discount rate. If the product has an end-of-life of less than three years, then you will have to estimate the volumes only until the end of the product's life.

- When calculating the cost of implementing an option you need to think about the cost of engineering change notices or requalification. Don't forget about costs like training, excess inventory, and other soft costs that would otherwise go unnoticed.

Technology. Does the option being considered provide us with a new or leading edge technology or does it draw us away from our technology road map? Don't forget to consider the supplier's road map as well. A decision that benefits you may hurt your supplier and move them in a direction that is not in their long-term interest.

Quality. Many times, changing a spec or reducing something to save money could affect the quality or perceived quality of the product or service. Not always, but it does need to be discussed and decided by a team. I've found that when the word "quality" is raised as a risk, the teams usually back off since it is a sacred cow to many companies. A word of caution is needed here. Many times, quality has been clearly overspecified by the design engineer or simply lifted off a previous specification. For example, a connector in the charging unit of a mobile phone may have a pull test requirement of 50,000. Reducing the pull test requirement from 50,000 to, say, 7,000 may, at first glance, appear to be a dramatic reduction in the level of quality and, thus, unacceptable. However, think about it. How many times do you charge your phone battery? Once, or even twice a day? That would make it 730 times a year, assuming that even when you are on vacation or sick in bed, you rush to charge your phone twice a day. How long do most people keep the same mobile phone? In order to withstand 50,000 pulls, the connector would have to be used for about 68 years. Quality should not be short-changed, but then again, it should not be used as a show-stopper without fully challenging the requirements and the *current application* of the product.

Manufacturing. Sometimes a strategy can not only save money but also shorten the manufacturing cycle or simplify the process, thereby improving yield. However, there are times when, in the name of cost savings, a team will decide to use a different material that may be less expensive but really messes up the manufacturing process and equipment. Clearly, before going ahead with a strategy that affects manufacturing, it is necessary to consult with your manufacturing manager and/or supplier.

Brand Image. There are numerous times when a team will come up with a strategy that reduces cost but will be shot down by marketing since it adversely affects the brand image of the company. For example, an annual report that few stockholders bother to read might be printed on the highest quality paper with numerous colors. A proposal to change the quality of paper or number of colors in order to save costs will likely be shot down by the public relations department since something like the annual report is viewed as a medium of projecting the company's image. Like a strategy that appears to reduce the quality or perceived quality of a product, such an argument has to be challenged, but it is equally important to understand marketing's perspective. Sometimes I advise teams to go to the next step (implementation) and start by addressing the risk of brand image by conducting a customer survey that may validate marketing's claim—or prove that it is unfounded.

Political. While it is clearly the goal of an AIM & DRIVE team to take cost out of the supply chain, there are times when a strategy is selected even though the savings are not that significant. For example, taking up the marketing case again, an option to move certain manufacturing processes from the United States to China may save a little money on the direct labor side, but may have a huge benefit by way of sales in China due to the local content. On the other hand, there could be the political risk of outsourcing business processes to India that can trigger a backlash in the United States as politicians make a convenient issue of the loss of white-collar jobs. The point is that a good team needs to weigh the political risk and benefit with the same degree of importance as the financial risk or benefit.

Flexibility. The team needs to ask itself whether a given strategy will save money today, only to lock the company into a certain investment, technology, or market. This lack of flexibility may come back to haunt them in the long run. On the other hand, a decision to move from a custom to standard material or process can have the benefit of an increase in flexibility or responsiveness. In this day of intense global competition, most world-class companies are looking for more flexibility so that they can respond quickly to changes in the marketplace.

Environmental. We live in a world that is getting more environmentally conscious. It would be poor strategy to ignore the environmental considerations when doing a risk-benefit analysis. A large chemical company that found a "cheaper" way to dispose of industrial waste had to spend hundreds of millions of dollars to ward off a spirited and annoying challenge from a notorious environmental group. This resulted in the chemical company's product being boycotted in many countries and tarnishing the company's image, affecting its other products as well. It does not mean that every strategy that affects the environment has to be scrapped. What it does mean is that the team recognizes the risk and *manages* it wisely. A good public relations program, an increased effort to minimize environmental risk, and education of the public will go a long way in avoiding the pitfalls that arise from failure to do the above. Many companies are joining forces with their customers and suppliers to create a "green" supply chain. The sooner a company gets on this bandwagon the better.

Delivery Performance. In their eagerness to save money, some teams forget the importance of consistently on-time delivery. This risk must be carefully evaluated before proceeding with a strategy to outsource a product or service. There are cases where the customer service has been moved off-shore along with the repairs and spare parts. While it may be possible (though not necessarily convenient) to talk with a technical service representative in another country, some customers would be very upset if, for example, they have to wait for a spare part that has to be flown in to the United States or Europe from China or India. A large retailer once decided to move from the existing, long-term, strategic supplier to a new one that offered a lower price. Everything went well until the peak holiday season when the supplier could not meet the spike in demand. Failure to deliver the required quantity in time resulted in a huge loss of market share and the retailer never quite recovered from that blow. On occasion a decision to go with a custom technology could jeopardize delivery performance, as a large provider of mobile phones found out in December 2003 when their supplier of cameras for a new handset failed to handle the unexpected surge in demand for camera phones.

Other Business Issues. Before concluding the risk-benefit analysis the team should ask itself, one last time, whether there are any other business-related issues that may not have been discussed. There are cases where none of the criteria above are at risk. However, it may be that a decision to switch from one supplier to another to save money results in the old supplier pulling out from selling you other products that they provide. And, these products may not be available elsewhere or only at a much higher price than what you are currently paying.

Quantitative and Qualitative Factors

Some benefits or risks may be quantifiable, while others may not. As mentioned earlier, all quantifiable savings should be carefully estimated and validated to the best of your ability. It has been my experience that many teams like to fudge the numbers to look good for their management. This is a practice that should be avoided, since it always catches up with you when you try to verify savings. When in doubt, use "to be determined" in the worksheet. In the example of Anything Inc., the strategy of increasing customer knowledge by creating in-house technicians for major accounts has clearly quantifiable savings, as measured by the reduction in number of field visits, which the team estimated to be $3.8 million. However, it is important to also acknowledge some qualitative savings like increase in customer satisfaction as well as risks like increase in employee turnover as well-trained employees find alternative opportunities.

Leveraging Ideas

A good team is one that can take a strategy statement, carefully evaluate constraints, and perform a well-rounded risk-benefit analysis—

and then proceed to execute the strategy. A world-class team is one that can not only execute the strategy but also find ways to leverage it across other product lines, businesses, and sometimes, other commodities. Some years ago I was working with a large computer manufacturer in Campinas, Brazil. The company invited six suppliers to participate in one of my AIM & DRIVE workshops. One of these suppliers provided facilities maintenance services totaling $800,000 a year. For a company the size of this computer manufacturer, $800,000 was a very small amount of money and I questioned the logic of inviting such a small supplier. I was told that the contract value may be small but the enthusiasm and cooperation of the supplier would make it worth our while to go through the process. Well, we did just that and the supplier came out with a really innovative idea that saved about 20 percent of the contract amount, or $160,000. Once again, this was pocket change for a multibillion-dollar company like this computer company.

A few months later I was conducting a similar workshop for the same company in the United States and this time the supplier was a larger facilities maintenance company with a contract of $40 million. After going through most of the exercise and coming up with token savings of around 5 percent, the team was ready to wrap up. I challenged them to consider the idea executed by the Campinas team. At first, the supplier fought it saying that this would not be possible. However, when the team leader contacted her colleague in Campinas she found out that the supplier's concerns were driven by self-interest and not the interest of the customer. The bottom line is that the U.S. team did, in fact, execute the same strategy and saved another $8 million. Soon, the global commodity team for facilities maintenance got involved and was able to leverage these savings around the other sites across the world, resulting in savings of tens of millions of dollars. All this was possible because one small supplier in a remote part of the world was open and creative with a strategy that was leveraged.

Let's make one thing very clear before we "leverage" ourselves into court. If an idea from a supplier is considered to be proprietary and the supplier makes it clear that this idea may not be shared even with other divisions of the customer company, then that request *must* be honored. All it takes is for a maverick team to share one supplier's proprietary idea with its competitor and that's the end of the AIM & DRIVE process. Some companies in the U.S. auto industry paid a heavy toll for "sharing" innovative but proprietary ideas between competing suppliers.

Prioritizing Strategies for Implementation

Sometimes a team may come up with many strategies that pass the risk-benefit test. It may be tempting to dive into implementing all the strategies at once. Be careful about biting off more than you can chew. In reality, most people already have their corporate plates full. I've found, from experience, that three or four strategies at a time are about as much as one team can handle. When prioritizing strategies for implementation it would seem obvious to take on those that show the maximum monetary benefit but that is not necessarily the best way to proceed. I've noticed that many managers seem to focus on short-term results. After all, that's how they are measured. So, be sensitive to the corporate situation and take on a couple of strategies that may not have the biggest savings potential, but that are easy and swift to execute. Also, take on those that do not require a major investment of funds or human resources since those tend to be put on the back burner while a decision is made to release the resources.

There really isn't any fixed rule as to how strategies should be prioritized: Experience has taught me that a strategy worth implementing should have all or most of the following qualities:

- Offers high potential savings.
- Offers high leverageable savings.

- Is relatively easy to execute.
- Can be executed rapidly.
- Addresses an immediate management initiative or directive.
- Offers clearly documentable savings (no fuzzy math).
- Addresses the goals of more than one interest group in the team.

Take a look at the strategy statements created by the Customer Service team at Anything Inc. (Figures 7-3 and 7-4). Note how the team took specific phrases from the list of strategic options (these are the words in italics), clearly articulated the strategic statements, and listed both quantitative and qualitative risks as well as benefits. In prioritizing the strategies for implementation, the team decided to focus on four strategy statements:

1. Increase *level of customer knowledge* by creating "in-house" service technicians for major accounts.
2. Change *level of customer expectation* to deal directly with TSC reps who will be authorized to ship replacement units directly to customers.
3. Improve *clarity of service manual* so customer is more knowledgeable.
4. Increase *skill of CS operator* in order to solve more problems over the telephone.

These statements were then entered on the Master Worksheet (Figure 7-5).

The Printed Manuals team at Anything Inc. took the following four functions or strategic options from their previous step (see Figure 6-7), created a strategy statement, and proceeded to perform a risk benefit analysis for each of them (see Figure 7-6).

(*text continues on page 156*)

Figure 7-3. Risk-benefit analysis worksheet for customer service for goods under warranty.

AIM & DRIVE: Reducing, Changing, or Eliminating Activities

PRIMARY COST : CUSTOMER SERVICE FOR GOODS UNDER WARRANTY

	STRATEGY STATEMENT	RISKS / COSTS	$ VALUE	BENEFITS	$ VALUE
1	Increase *clarity of task* to reduce field technician's time at the customer's site.	More questions for customer to answer		Eliminate non-value added time during field visits	$240,000
		Increase call time	$160,000	Quicker turnaround	
				Increased customer satisfaction	
	Priority (H/M/L) : L				
	Net Savings : $80,000		$160,000		$240,000
	KEY COST DRIVER : Field Service Efficiency				
	CONSTRAINTS : Turnaround time for existing customers cannot go beyond 48 hours				
2	Increase *level of customer knowledge* by creating an "in-house" service technician for major accounts.	Training costs	$400,000	Increase customer satisfaction	$40,000
		Employee turnover		Fewer CS calls	$200,000
		Lack of control		Fewer TSC calls	$3,840,000
		Customer perception of quality of service		Fewer field visits	
	Priority (H/M/L) : H				
	Net Savings : $3,680,000		$400,000		$4,080,000
	KEY COST DRIVER : Field Service Efficiency				
	CONSTRAINTS : Turnaround time for existing customers cannot go beyond 48 hours				
3	Change *level of customer expectation* to deal directly with TSC reps who will be authorized to ship replacement units directly to customers.	Customer dissatisfaction		Fewer field visits	$11,520,000
		Freight costs	$1,000,000	Quicker response time	
		Customer training costs	$100,000	Increased customer satisfaction	
		Higher TSC service costs	$5,000,000		
		Management buy-in			
		More documentation	$100,000		
	Priority (H/M/L) : H				
	Net Savings : $5,320,000		$6,200,000		$11,520,000
	KEY COST DRIVER : Technical Service Center Efficiency				
	CONSTRAINTS : Turnaround time for existing customers cannot go beyond 48 hours				

Figure 7-4. Risk-benefit analysis worksheet for customer service for goods under warranty (continued).

AIM & DRIVE: Reducing, Changing, or Eliminating Activities

PRIMARY COST : CUSTOMER SERVICE FOR GOODS UNDER WARRANTY

	STRATEGY STATEMENT	RISKS / COSTS	$ VALUE	BENEFITS	$ VALUE
4	*Improve clarity of the service manual* to increase customer's knowledge	Cost to redesign	$50,000	Customer solves more problems	
		New manual may not be used		Fewer CS calls	$200,000
		Old manual rendered obsolete		Fewer TSC calls	$200,000
				Fewer field visits	$200,000
	Priority (H/M/L) : H				
	Net Savings : $550,000		$50,000		$600,000
	KEY COST DRIVER : Technical Service Center Efficiency				
	CONSTRAINTS : Turaround time for existing customers cannot go beyond 48 hours				
5	Reduce *level of TSC workload* by hiring new TSC technicians.	Hiring costs	$10,000	More cases solved by TSC = fewer field visits	$576,000
		Higher payroll costs	$150,000	More customers served	
		More space required		Quicker response time	
		Higher training costs	$3,000	Increased customer satisfaction	
	Priority (H/M/L) : M				
	Net Savings : $413,000		$163,000		$576,000
	KEY COST DRIVER : Technical Service Center Efficiency				
	CONSTRAINTS : Turaround time for existing customers cannot go beyond 48 hours				
6	Increase the *skill levels of CS operators* to solve more problems over the telephone.	Training costs	$50,000	Fewer TSC calls	$200,000
		Hiring costs	$20,000	Fewer field visits	$1,500,000
		Increased labor costs	$75,000	Greater customer satisfaction	
		Increased telephone costs			
		Customer perception of quality of service			
	Priority (H/M/L) : H				
	Net Savings : $1,555,000		$145,000		$1,700,000
	KEY COST DRIVER : Customer Service Efficiency				
	CONSTRAINTS : Turaround time for existing customers cannot go beyond 48 hours				

Figure 7-5. Master worksheet for customer service for goods under warranty.

AIM & DRIVE: Master Worksheet

A PRIMARY COST : CUSTOMER SERVICE FOR GOODS UNDER WARRANTY

Total Spend = $23,206,000

CRITICAL COSTS	COST DRIVERS	KEY COST DRIVERS	SELECTED STRATEGY STATEMENT	ACTION ITEMS	WHO	DUE DATE
I	M	D	R	I	VE	VE VE
Field Service Labor	FS labor rate FS efficiency TSC efficiency CS efficiency unit call rate	FS labor rate (# of hrs / visit call) FS efficiency (# of visit calls / # of calls to TSC) TSC efficiency (# of calls to TSC / # of calls to CS)	Increase level of customer knowledge by creating an "in-house" service technician for major accounts.			
Direct Material	unit price new part requirement repair effectiveness defect rate		Change level of customer expectation to deal directly with TSC reps who will be authorized to ship replacement units directly to customers.			
Freight	freight rate part weight shipment size					
			Improve clarity of the service manual to increase customer's knowledge.			
			Increase the skill levels of CS operators to solve more problems over the telephone.			

Figure 7-6. Risk-benefit analysis worksheet for printed manuals.

AIM & DRIVE: Reducing, Changing, or Eliminating Activities

PRIMARY COST : PRINTED MANUALS

	STRATEGY STATEMENT	RISKS / COSTS	$ VALUE	BENEFITS	$ VALUE
1	Reduce the *number of features* pre-loaded on the Zigmo thereby reducing the number of printed pages by 25%	Some customers dissatisfied		Lower paper costs	$2,056,000
		Fewer features to market		Lower printing, translation costs	$208,000
				Lower freight cost	$192,000
				Reduced cycle time	
	Priority (H/M/L) : M				
	Net Savings : $2,456,000		$0		$2,456,000
	KEY COST DRIVER : Level of detail				
	CONSTRAINTS : Marketing: Any changes made to the manual would have to be completed in 6 months to ensure the smooth introduction of the new Zigmo model				
2	Reduce the *percent of information* on other media by printing only the Quick Start Guide and having the rest of the manual available online	Some customers dissatisfied		Dramatic reduction in paper, printing, and translation costs	$6,560,000
		Accessability of information if computer goes down		Improves company image	
		Paul Schultz does not buy-in		Environmentally friendlier	
		Cost to develop Internet access	$500,000	Provides a competitive advantage	$500,000
				Improves time-to-market	
				Improves portability of the unit	
				Reduced cycle time	
	Priority (H/M/L) : M				
	Net Savings : $6,060,000		$500,000		$6,560,000
	KEY COST DRIVER : Level of detail				
	CONSTRAINTS : Marketing: Any changes made to the manual would have to be completed in 6 months to ensure the smooth introduction of the new Zigmo model				

#				$2,500,000
3	For a *number of customers with several Zigmos* purchased, provide 1 set of manuals for every 5 Zigmos	Some customers dissatisfied (manuals are not accessible to users when they need	*Lower cost of Customer Manuals*	
		Increased process costs	Customers not required to store manuals	$100,000
			Greater customer satisfaction	
	Priority (H/M/L) : M			
	Net Savings : $2,400,000		$100,000	$2,500,000

KEY COST DRIVER : Doc requirement
CONSTRAINTS : Marketing: Any changes made to the manual would have to be completed in 6 months to ensure the smooth introduction of the new Zigmo model

#				$4,111,800
4	Change *grade of paper* from glossy to non-glossy paper	May not be as aesthetically pleasing	Reduction in paper cost of approximately	
		Possible resistance from Paul Schultz	Environmentally more friendly	
		May result in ink bleed		
	Priority (H/M/L) : M			
	Net Savings : $4,111,800		$0	$4,111,800

KEY COST DRIVER : Paper price
CONSTRAINTS : Marketing: Any changes made to the manual would have to be completed in 6 months to ensure the smooth introduction of the new Zigmo model

1. Number of features preloaded on machine

2. Percent of information on other media

3. Number of customers with several Zigmos

4. Grade of paper

What one can learn from this team is that some of the options are not mutually exclusive. For example, strategy statement #2 in Figure 7-6 calls for the elimination of most of the printed material by putting all the content, except for the Quick Start Guide, on-line. It also has the highest potential savings of $6 million. If that option were to be chosen, it would mean that the other three strategies would not have the same impact as if they were implemented independently. That is perfectly acceptable. What the team has to do is carefully examine the mutual exclusivity and determine whether they are going with one strategy at the expense of the others or whether they would like to run another strategy or a combination of the other strategies.

The Corrugated Boxes team decided to focus on two strategic options, namely the *number of pallet alternatives* and the *type of middle liner* for the box (see Figure 7-7). These were shown in Figure 6-9 in the previous chapter. They took the first option and created two strategy statements around it. The first was a bold idea of completely eliminating the pallets altogether. If that were successful the second strategy, which was to stack more boxes on a pallet, would be moot. The team also intended to reduce the middle liner board from 26 lbs. performance to 23 lbs. performance. Now, here is something that should be noted carefully. For both elimination of pallets and reduction in the middle liner board thickness, the savings calculated were just ten and nine cents, respectively. On a volume of around 1,100,000 boxes a year this would hardly be called a breakthrough strategy. However, the team was confident that if these strategies were successfully implemented on the Zigmo product line, they could be

Figure 7-7. Risk-benefit analysis worksheet for corrugated boxes.

AIM & DRIVE: Reducing, Changing, or Eliminating Activities

PRIMARY COST : CORRUGATED BOXES

STRATEGY STATEMENT	RISKS / COSTS	$ VALUE	BENEFITS	$ VALUE
1 Increase the *# of pallet alternatives* by eliminating pallets	Possible quality loss resulting in damage (forklift)		Cost savings of $0.10 per box (.10 x 1,100,000). Replicable to all (15) boxes.	$1,650,000
	Possible safety issue		Savings in freight cost	$265,000
	Water damage (water on ground)		Saving natural resources and land fill	
	Additional cost of stronger bubble-wrap	$165,000		
Priority (H/M/L) :　　　H				
Net Savings :　$1,750,000		$165,000		$1,915,000
KEY COST DRIVER : Pallet utilization CONSTRAINTS :				
2 Increase the *# of pallet alternatives* by double-stacking bale packs			Cost savings of $0.05 per box. Replicable to all (15) boxes.	$825,000
Strategy will be put on hold pending outcome of other two strategies			Better truck utilization (10 boxes x 34 = 5% of freight). Replicable to all (15) boxes.	$57,600
Priority (H/M/L) :　　　M				
Net Savings :　$882,600		$0		$882,600
KEY COST DRIVER : Pallet utilization CONSTRAINTS :				
3 Change *type of middle liner* from 26-lb performance to 23-lb performance	Lower compression strength		23-lb performance saves $0.09 per box. Replicable to all (15) boxes.	$1,485,000
	Reduction in safety margin			
Priority (H/M/L) :　　　H				
Net Savings :　$1,485,000		$0		$1,485,000
KEY COST DRIVER : Liner price CONSTRAINTS :				

implemented over other products sold by Anything Inc., with total volumes of fifteen times that of the Zigmo line. It was estimated that the leveraged strategies would save around $3.4 million.

With the selection of precise strategy statements, it is now time to develop action plans for each strategy. We will discuss this in the next chapter.

Checklist for Step 5: Reducing, Changing, or Eliminating Activities That Cause Cost

❏ Review the Risk-Return model and think about which box most appropriately describes the project under discussion.

❏ Identify and discuss constraints, if any.

❏ Take the top four or five options and create a strategy statement for each of them with a verb in front and an explanation after each phrase from the list of options.

❏ Discuss and develop a list of risks and benefits from different perspectives for each strategy statement.

❏ Quantify those risks and benefits that can be quantified.

❏ Discuss if any of the benefits can be leveraged and the expected value of the leveraged benefit.

❏ Determine whether strategies are mutually exclusive or not.

❏ Prioritize the selected strategies for implementation.

❏ Enter the results in the Master Worksheet.

Implementing an Action Plan

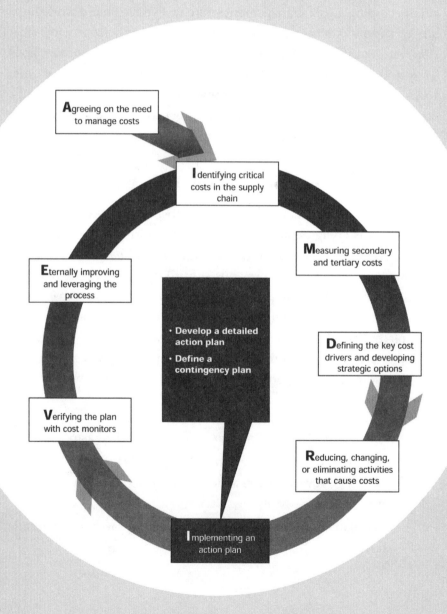

How many times have you attended meetings, discussed issues, debated alternatives, and come up with a plan only to see it fall by the wayside as just another idea that was never implemented? I cannot tell you how frustrating it is to suppliers in particular. It takes a lot for a supplier to open up to a customer and agree to collaborate on developing a cost management strategy. I've facilitated workshops where suppliers have worked diligently and openly to provide what one would call breakthrough solutions. Then, the customer goes away and does nothing. Sometimes this is attributed to lack of time, too many fires to fight, or the "not invented here" syndrome. Mostly, strategies are not implemented simply because there was no clear implementation plan. Well, it's time to correct that.

Ingredients for a Good Implementation Plan

An implementation plan does not have to be complex. All you are looking for is an agreement on the three Ws and it is not the World-Wide Web I am talking about. It is *what*, *who*, and *when*. The strategy statements selected in the previous step represent *how* the team intends to reduce, eliminate, or change those activities that cause costs. For each such strategy statement it is essential to develop a clear action plan. That should be pretty straightforward, right? Wrong. Too often, teams try to rush through this part of the process. A good action plan has some basic ingredients or rules that the team is well advised to follow:

1. The action plan should be as clear and detailed as possible.
2. The risks that were listed in the previous step of the process should be reviewed and action items in the plan must address those risks.
3. The plan should be feasible and agreed upon by all members of the team.

4. Responsibility should be accepted by individuals present at the strategy meeting/s.

5. Completion dates should be specific and agreed upon by the person/s accepting responsibility for each action item.

6. There must be a contingency plan in case the original strategy does not work.

7. The plan should be "sold" correctly to the stakeholders.

Let's explore these guidelines one by one.

Create Clear and Detailed Action Plans

In general, I recommend erring on the side of being too detailed with the action plan. Imagine that you are writing code for a software program. Garbage in—garbage out. It is really important to list all the little details because it's surprisingly easy for a team to lose its way in the implementation stage of the process. You see, when a team is strategizing over the first six steps, the various players work together typically in a face-to-face meeting or workshop. Once they finish Step 6 of the AIM & DRIVE process—**R**educing, changing, or eliminating activities that cause costs—they tend to go back to their respective jobs and the momentum is lost. Good project planning can prevent brilliant ideas from falling through the cracks. Notice how the Customer Service team at Anything Inc. listed the actions for each strategy statement (Figure 8-1).

Take the first statement:

Increase the level of customer knowledge by creating in-house service technicians for major accounts.

It would be easy to list a couple of action steps like:

• Identify technicians.

• Train technicians.

• Technicians conduct in-house repairs.

Figure 8-1. Implementation plan worksheet for customer service for goods under warranty.

AIM & DRIVE: Implementing an Action Plan			
PRIMARY COST : CUSTOMER SERVICE FOR GOODS UNDER WARRANTY			
SELECTED STRATEGY	ACTION ITEM	WHO	DUE DATE
	Identify key customers	Mktg	1-Jun
	Send rep to customer for preliminary meeting	Mktg	8-Jun
Increase level of customer	Select target customer personnel for training	Mktg	15-Jun
knowledge by creating an "in-	Perform in-house training	Mktg, Fixit	8-Jul
2 house" service technician for	Co-locate Fixit technician for trial run	Fixit	15-Jul
major accounts.	Verify performance of in-house tech	Mktg, Fixit	8-Aug
Net Savings: $3,680,000	In-house tech performs repairs alone	Fixit in-house tech	15-Aug
	Survey key customers and obtain feedback	Mktg	1-Jul
Change customer expectation	Tabulate results	Mktg	8-Jul
to deal directly with TSC reps	Confirm changes in freight and inventory costs	Mfg, Eng, Proc, Fin, Fixit	15-Jul
3 who will be authorized to ship	Presentation to management	Mfg, Eng, Proc, Fin, Fixit	22-Jul
replacement units directly to	Train TSC personnel	Fixit	10-Aug
customers. Net Savings: $5,320,000	Implement new policy on shipping parts to customers	Mktg, Fixit	15-Aug
	Analyze historic complaints to identify recurring problems	Eng, Fixit	15-Jun
Improve clarity of the service	Red line current manual	Eng, QA, Mfg	28-Jun
4 manual to increase customer's	Prepare new manual	Eng, Fixit	28-Jul
knowledge.	Print trial run and test with key customers	Mktg, Print	10-Aug
	Print trial version after any revisions	Eng, Fixit, Mktg, Adm, Print	17-Aug
Net Savings: $550,000	Distribute new manual to existing customers	Mktg	31-Aug
	Analyze historic list of complaints to identify problems solvable over the phone by non-technical people	Eng, Mktg, Fixit	15-Jun
Increase the skill levels of CS operators to solve more	Develop training program for CS operators	Mktg, Eng	30-Jun
6 problems over the telephone.	Train existing CS operators	Mktg, Eng	30-Jul
Net Savings: $1,555,000	Develop reference booklet of common questions & answers for CS operators	Mktg, Eng, Fixit, Adm	31-Aug

Instead, the team recognized that the success of such an initiative depended on the cooperation of key customers and hence felt it necessary to first identify those customers. Once that was done a representative from Anything Inc. would visit each key customer to brief them on the benefits of having an in-house technician and to solicit their cooperation. Why would a customer want to enter into such a program? Its one of those "what's in it for me" issues. A case would have to be made that this will save the customer time in getting the product fixed, lessen user/customer frustration, and increase the Zigmo's productivity for that customer. Some customers may see the benefit while others may not. For those who agree, the next step would be to select some key personnel from the customer who could perform such in-house repairs. Once that is done, a training program has to be developed and the in-house technicians trained and certified by either Anything Inc. or Fixit, as the case may be. Before letting the newly trained personnel go off and start performing repairs of Zigmos that fail, it would be wise to place an experienced technician from Fixit at the customer's site to monitor the newly trained customer's in-house technician during a trial run. Once the experienced technician is satisfied that the in-house technician is ready to handle the basic repairs on his/her own, a final certificate can be issued and the in-house technician can perform repairs independently.

Address Risks from the Previous Step

In a team's hurry to complete the implementation plan, it is quite normal to ignore a very important factor, the risks that were discussed as part of the risk-benefit analysis in the previous step. Clearly the risks do not disappear just because they are outweighed by the benefits. When I am asked to evaluate AIM & DRIVE teams on their cost management strategy, I wait for them to get to this part. After they have presented what they think is a terrific implementation plan, all I do is read out a couple of risks from their Risk-Benefit Worksheet and ask the simple question, "How have you addressed these risks or have you assumed that they would just disappear if you ignored them long enough?" You should see the face on the person making the presentation. Brilliant teams with brilliant ideas, and yet, they ignore something as basic as this! It is strongly recommended that the team review each and every risk for the respective strategy statements and make sure that these risks are addressed in the action plan. In some cases, a risk can be eliminated or at least reduced by taking one action or another.

Look at the team working on the printed user manual. The specifications call for a very expensive grade of glossy paper and multicolor printing. The critical cost is the cost of paper. One of the key cost drivers is the *price of paper.* A strategic option chosen by the team is to replace the glossy paper with regular paper. It was expected that this would save the company almost 50 percent of the cost of the manual, and with the volume being discussed, that was a few million dollars. While doing the risk-benefit analysis, one of the team members pointed out that the original spec for glossy paper had come from marketing, who believed that it was important to project an image. Besides, for reasons best known to them, the cost of the service manual came out of marketing's budget. Paul Schultz, the creative director, was very proud of his design of the manual, including the high-quality paper and numerous colors. So, in the risk section you may have noticed in Figure 7-6 there was a statement that read, "Possible resistance from Paul Schultz." When the team presented their implementation plan it seemed pretty straightforward:

- Identify alternative, low-cost paper grades and supplier.
- Obtain samples from supplier.
- Evaluate samples and choose alternative paper.
- Issue change order to supplier.
- Phase out stock of glossy paper.
- Incorporate new paper stock into manuals.

Not a word about how the team would win over Paul Schultz. The team was politely asked whether anyone had actually talked with Paul about this and the reply was, "We certainly have and were told that a majority of customers preferred the glossy paper and multicolor printing. However, once he sees how much money we will save, he cannot but agree with our strategy." We managed to convince the team to address the risk in their action plan and think of a way to minimize or eliminate it. In Figure 8-2 it will be noticed that the team

Figure 8-2. Implementation plan worksheet for printed manuals.

AIM & DRIVE: Implementing an Action Plan			
PRIMARY COST : PRINTED MANUALS			
SELECTED STRATEGY	ACTION ITEM	WHO	DUE DATE
1 Reduce the number of features pre-loaded on the Zigmo (This strategy will be implemented only if Strategy 2 fails) Net Savings : $ 2,456,000	Conduct survey to study impact on customer satisfaction	Marketing	15-Aug
	Evaluate survey results and make decision to go/no go	Mktg.	20-Aug
	If go, take relevant feature/section out of the Zigmo/manual	Mktg. / Eng. / Manuf.	20-Sep
2 Print only the Quick Start Guide and have the rest of the manual available on-line. (This strategy is to be attempted first because of the highest potential gain and taking into account future trends in user manuals.) Net Savings : $ 6,060,000	Customer survey to study impact on customer satisfaction	Marketing	21-Jun
	Determine number of manuals needed in hard copy	Marketing	28-Jun
	Prepare cost estimate of putting the manuals on-line	Mktg. / Proc. / Eng.	10-Jul
	Make buy-in presentation to Paul Schultz	Mktg. / Proc. / Eng.	15-Jul
	If approved by Paul, redesign manuals to enhance graphics	Marketing	15-Sep
	Design/develop Internet site	Mktg. / Eng.	31-Oct
	Design troubleshooting guide for back panel of Zigmo	Mktg. / Eng. / Manuf.	31-Oct
	Implement process changes to include the above	Manufacturing	30-Nov
	Implement "800" number for customer service	Marketing	30-Nov
3 For customers that purchase several Zigmos, provide 1 set of manuals for every 5 Zigmos (This strategy will be implemented only if Strategy 2 fails) Net Savings : $ 2,400,000	Evaluate the impact on process costs	Logistics / Mktg. / Manuf.	15-Jun
	Identify customers with purchases of multiple Zigmos	Marketing	15-Jun
	Educate customers about the option of getting fewer manuals	Marketing	20-Jun
	Redesign current process to allow for fewer manuals per set	Manuf. / Mktg. / Logistics	15-Jul
	Ship required number of manuals per set	Marketing	31-Jul
4 Change from glossy to non-glossy paper (This strategy will be implemented only if Strategy 2 fails) Net Savings : $ 4,111,800	Identify alternative, low cost paper grades and supplier	Procurement	10-Jun
	Obtain samples from supplier	Procurement	15-Jun
	Evaluate samples and choose a couple of alternative types of lower grade paper	Marketing/Manuf.	25-Jun
	Print samples of manual with at least 2 alternative grades of paper	Supplier	10-Jul
	Conduct random survey of existing and potential customers	Marketing	31-Jul
	Tabulate results, present alternate solution to Paul Schultz	Marketing/ Procurement	8-Aug
	If approved, execute changeover process to new type of paper	Procurement	15-Sep

did address the issue of Paul Schultz, even though it was agreed that this strategy of changing the type of paper would be implemented only if the first priority of putting most of the manual on-line failed to meet with Paul's approval. Here's what they came up with:

- Identify alternative, low-cost paper grades and supplier.
- Obtain samples from supplier.
- Evaluate samples and choose a couple of alternative types of lower grade paper.

- Print samples of manual with at least two alternative grades of paper.
- Conduct random survey of existing and potential customers showing them the current manual with glossy paper and the two alternatives asking whether they:
  a) Preferred glossy paper?
  b) Preferred alternative #1?
  c) Preferred alternative #2?
  d) Did not care which grade of paper was used?
  e) Read the manual?
  f) Removed the shrinkwrap from the manual?
- Tabulate results and, if change is recommended, present results with alternate solution to Paul Schultz.
- Obtain buy-in from Paul and marketing team.
- If buy-in obtained, issue change order to supplier.
- Phase out stock of glossy paper.
- Incorporate new paper stock into manuals.

Regardless of whether the team decided to implement this strategy or not, see how detailed this action item list is and how the risk has been mitigated by clear action steps? As it turned out, the results of the survey were shocking to Paul. It showed that 97 percent of users did not care and a staggering 76 percent did not even remove the shrinkwrap from the user manual. Taking these results to Paul along with the recommended changes and accompanying cost savings ensured that the strategy was approved.

The Corrugated Boxes team also faced a similar issue as the other two teams. In their risk-benefit analysis they listed the risk of damage to the Zigmos caused by a forklift if pallets were to be eliminated. However, in their implementation plan they did not address the issue of product damage. With the right feedback during their presentation, the team decided to investigate different types of bubble wrap that could withstand a bit rougher handling than the current one. They even went back to the previous step and quantified the additional cost of the new bubble wrap. It should be noticed in the Implementation Worksheet (Figure 8-3), for the second strategy statement—*change type of middle liner from 26-lb performance to 23-lb performance*— the team decided to end the action plan with the statement, *if tests are positive, initiate changeover process.* Some teams choose to write the entire changeover process in their AIM & DRIVE Implementation Worksheet. Others, like the Corrugated Boxes team, preferred to refer to an existing changeover sequence and did not feel it necessary to write the whole process down again. Each team will develop its own style, and that's as it should be.

Figure 8-3. Implementation plan worksheet for corrugated boxes.

AIM & DRIVE: Implementing an Action Plan			
PRIMARY COST : CORRUGATED BOXES			
SELECTED STRATEGY	ACTION ITEM	WHO	DUE DATE
1 Increase the # of pallet alternatives by eliminating pallets	Analysis of product list to see which ones the strategy can be applied on	Account manager	21-Jun
	Run pilot order with supplier on next Zigmo order without pallets	Account manager	28-Jul
	Test different types of bubble wrap that can withstand fork lift damage	Packaging engineer	10-Jul
	Evaluate and make Go /No Go decision	Packaging engineer	15-Jul
	If go, then execute across all shipments	Account manager	15-Aug
Net Savings : $ 1,750,000			
3 Change type of middle liner from 26-lb performance to 23-lb performance	Gather samples of 23-lb. performance packaging	Procurement	28-Jun
	Meet with packaging engineers to review whether compression strength can be changed and that safety factor is realistic	Procurement	15-Jul
	Establish minimum requirements; conduct compression tests	Packaging engineer	31-Jul
	If tests are positive, initiate changeover process	Account manager	31-Aug
Net Savings : $ 1,485,000			

Confirm Feasibility of the Action Plan

There is no point preparing an action plan unless it has a chance of being fully implemented. Make sure that all views are heard and discussed. In some cases I have seen action plans include steps that were not discussed in the risk-benefit analysis. For example, when moving from one type of material to another, a team may have evaluated the benefits of the new material and the costs of switching over. However, while preparing the action plan they realize that the supplier will need to make samples of the product with the new material and that the samples will need to be approved by the customer's engineers. Two issues may make this impractical. First, the supplier may not have the budget to produce the samples and, second, the customer's engineers may not have time to test and qualify the new parts since they are busy working on new products. It does not mean that the strategy should be immediately abandoned. Rather, it points out that the team should go back to the previous step and redo the risk-benefit analysis.

Assign Responsibility and Determine Time Lines

Once action plans have been vetted by the team it is necessary to assign responsibilities for each action. It may not always be the case that the person responsible for the execution of a certain action item is present at the meeting. In such cases it is best that a person present at the meeting take the responsibility of ensuring that the action item is communicated to the person who will ultimately execute it. There are times when an action item will have two or more people responsible, in which case all those persons should sign off and are equally responsible.

Time lines should then be discussed. Be realistic and make sure that there is agreement from the person owning responsibility for that particular action item. Some teams prefer to set time lines in days or weeks from the date of the meeting. I recommend that you enter a calendar date where possible. This makes it much easier for the coordinator of the implementation plan to remind respective members when his/her action item is due or late. There are times when someone may commit to a certain date and later realize that it was too ambitious or unrealistic. In such cases it is better to inform the project coordinator and have the date moved. The coordinator would then look at the other activities and revise the implementation time line if necessary. It's much better to do this than to have people waiting for an action item and get upset with the person who is delaying the successful implementation of a strategy.

Develop Contingency Plans

Not every action plan will go the way you expect. Since a lot is riding on the success of an action plan, it doesn't make sense to give up on an idea just because of a roadblock here or there. Remember the analogy of a river in Sun Tzu's *Art of War,* presented in Chapter 3? When a river, on its way to its ultimate goal of emptying itself into an ocean, sea, or larger body of water, runs into a hard bed of rock, what does it do? It looks for an alternative path to get around the obstacle. It uses the path of least resistance and meanders either right or left. But it does manage to get back on track to its destination. So too, a good action plan should be flexible and adapt to change in order to overcome roadblocks. Remember, it is not the specific option you choose but the *ultimate goal* that matters. Unlike a river, a team has an opportunity to evaluate alternatives *before* running into a roadblock or obstacle.

I remember taking a course in Leadership and Management from a former Stanford professor and management consultant. He gave us a case study that emphasized the importance of integrating a contingency plan and implementation plan. Take a look at this case:

Case Study: A Journey to the Moon

You are a member of a space program that is attempting to put the first human beings on the moon in the twenty-first century. A spacecraft carrying six astronauts has reached the outer orbit around the moon. Two astronauts were sent down to the moon in a smaller module while four others stayed on the Mother Ship. The landing was perfect and the two astronauts who landed on its surface were able to collect samples and do certain experiments. Data collected from the experiments were sent over to the Mother Ship but could not be sent to earth (this is a case-imposed constraint). The samples collected were tucked safely into the lunar module. Communication with the Mother Ship was not very clear but a distinct *wow!* from the two astronauts was heard, before they took off from the moon's surface. According to plan, the lunar module lifted off from the moon and went into a lower orbit to get a few more pictures. After circling the moon a few times the astronauts prepared to blast out of the lower orbit to dock with the Mother Ship, which was orbiting at a higher altitude. That's when something went wrong. The rockets that were supposed to fire the lunar module out of the lower orbit did not ignite.

You and your team at Mission Control are most concerned about this and go through a drill to get those rockets to fire. You try everything but nothing works. Time is running out and a decision has to be made. Your team begins to evaluate a couple of strategic options:

Option #1: Attempt to rescue the two astronauts. Have the Mother Ship use its power to blast out of its current orbit and dock with the lunar module at the lower orbit, transfer the two astronauts and the samples, circle the moon a few more times, then use the remaining power to blast out of that orbit and head back to earth. The problem is the Mother Ship may not have the power to do all this and, besides, docking at the lower orbit is expected to be extremely dangerous. The probability of success calculated by your team is 20 percent. "Success" means that the Mother Ship returns to earth with all six astronauts, the data, and all samples. There was an 80 percent chance of failure, which would mean the death of all six astronauts, no samples, and no data.

Option #2: Abandon the lunar module and the two astronauts and head back home. This has a 90 percent probability of success but means that while four astronauts and the data would be back on earth with the Mother Ship, it was certain that the mission would lose two astronauts and the samples.

What a tough decision for you and your team! You have *five* minutes to make this call and the commander of the Mother Ship is not allowed to make this decision. It is up to *you*.

So, what would you do?

I've seen this case play out in a number of ways. Some teams argue about probability theory while others talk about individual goals versus team goals versus organizational goals. Still others discuss a more holistic approach about the overall objective. There has been vigorous debate and I've even witnessed team members accusing others in their team of being cold-hearted on the one hand or soft on the other.

Is there a right or wrong answer? I don't think so. What I do know is that if I were asked to make this call my decision would be, "Execute the contingency plan we already have." Decisions to go one way or the other if the primary strategy runs into problems should not be made on the spur of the moment when there is strong emotion, insufficient data, and lack of time. A good team thinks about the many probable ways the strategy could be derailed and discusses various alternatives or contingencies they will follow if one or the other strategy becomes impossible to execute. In all such cases the process guidelines are fairly similar.

- Think of the desired goal and keep focused on that goal. It answers the question *why?*
- Review the risks in your risk-benefit analysis. They will usually give you reasons why something could go wrong.
- Look over your strategic options and examine which other option would get you to your goal.
- Rewrite the implementation plan to include the new action items should the team have to put in place a contingency plan.

In the case study presented above, if the contingency plan was to abandon the two astronauts and return home, then there would have to be an implementation plan in place to address the certain backlash from the press and public. In other words, the focus would have to be more on a public relations campaign and much of this would have been prepared before the Mother Ship left earth.

If the contingency plan was to attempt a rescue of the two astronauts in the lunar module then the implementation plan would focus on getting the best team of experts in place in the shortest possible time to help execute a difficult plan regardless of cost or protocol.

In the language of AIM & DRIVE, a contingency plan for a given strategy would be one of the following:

- Use another strategic option for the same cost driver.
- Choose another cost driver for the same critical cost.
- Stick to the same strategy but use a different implementation plan.

Take the example of the printed manuals. The team initially did not have a customer survey in its implementation plan. They expected to approach Paul Schultz with the cost savings from changing the quality of paper and assumed that he would buy in on that idea. What would the contingency plan be if Paul Schultz refused to authorize the change in paper quality? Remember, the critical cost is *paper*, the key cost driver is the *paper price*, and one of the strategic options is reducing the *quality* of paper.

One contingency would be to drop the idea of changing the quality of paper to get a lower price but focus on the paper source, volumes, stability of order, and better negotiation strategy. This would also help reduce the value of the key cost driver, paper price.

A second option would be to use another cost driver for the same critical cost, if the paper price could not be reduced by a change in the quality of paper. If one were to look at the detailed formula and list the cost drivers for the cost of paper in a user manual, the *number of pages* stands out as a distinct possibility for reduction. This could be a strategy in itself that could run parallel with the strategy to change the quality of paper. Or, it could be used as a contingency if Paul Schultz shoots down the idea of using a different quality of paper.

Finally, a contingency plan could be the original plan but implemented differently. In the printed manual example, the original plan of getting Paul Schultz's support may not be achieved if Paul digs his heels in. Rather than abandon that goal, the team may have a contingency in place that called for a meeting with the Chief Financial Officer, to present the market survey, the monetary benefits of switching paper type, and any other issues that may help the CFO override Paul's decision.

While developing their contingency plan (Figure 8-4), the Customer Service team at Anything Inc. used an interesting combination

Figure 8-4. Contingency plan worksheet for customer service for goods under warranty.

AIM & DRIVE: Developing a Contingency Plan		
PRIMARY COST : CUSTOMER SERVICE FOR GOODS UNDER WARRANTY		
SELECTED STRATEGY STATEMENT	DESIRED GOAL	CONTINGENCY PLAN What alternative strategy will you implement if the desired goal cannot be achieved by the proposed Strategic Option ?
2 Increase level of customer knowledge by creating an "in-house" service technician for major accounts.	In-house technician helps customer solve problem	Further training / Replace unit
3 Change level of customer expectation to deal directly with TSC reps who will be authorized to ship replacement units directly to customers.	Avoid sending field rep to customer	Provide incentives to customer
4 Improve clarity of the service manual to increase customer's knowledge.	Customer solves problem	Implement training program for key customers
6 Increase the skill levels of CS operators to solve more problems over the telephone.	Solve more problems at Customer Service Center	Redefine scope of work and hire more qualified operators

of the suggestions made above. For their first strategy: *increase the level of customer knowledge by creating "in-house" service technicians for major customers*, the desired goal is to have the in-house service technician solve the problem at the customer's site. If that was found to not make much of a difference, the team felt that the same goal could still be achieved either by providing more training to the technicians (same strategy but implemented differently) or authorize replacement of the unit itself (another strategic option for the same goal).

Selling the Plan to Stakeholders

In the many years that I have facilitated AIM & DRIVE strategy sessions, I have seen so many cases where teams have worked hard to come up with innovative cost management strategies only to see their ideas gather dust on the shelf. Why does this happen? The only reason I can see is that the team failed to "sell" their strategy to the right stakeholders and get their collective buy-in. Many a time it is the lack of management support; often it is the "not invented here" syndrome of the stakeholders. And, on a few occasions, it is due to a really bad presentation made by the team to its management or stakeholders. Having come so far it is only appropriate to prepare a "buy-in" strategy to take the team over the top. Here is a list of things that I advise a team to do if they intend to get this buy-in.

- Obtain additional input as needed.
- Review and revise worksheets.
- Identify target audience.
- Gather information about the audience.
- Anticipate management concerns.
- Prepare sales presentation.
- Make the "best" presenters do the presentation.

In most cases, despite their best efforts, the team will tend to go through the AIM & DRIVE process, making numerous *assumptions* along the way. Many times costs are estimated, the values of cost drivers are not actually calculated, savings are approximated, or time lines on the implementation plan are guesstimates. It is important to obtain additional input as needed to validate your assumptions, calculations, or decisions.

Go back and review your worksheets. Make sure that there is a clear thread through the process and that you are comfortable with the strategic options chosen, that you have identified all possible risks that may be encountered and all the benefits that could be leveraged and all the contingencies that could bail your team out if the strategy runs aground. Once you have done all that, it may be necessary to revise some of the worksheets.

Now it is time for the team to identify who would be the right audience for a presentation of its strategy. Very few companies that I have worked with will have all the decision makers present on the AIM & DRIVE team. Nokia is probably the only exception in my experience. That is why they have been able to gain a competitive edge on others since the time taken to implement a strategy is much shorter than any other company I have worked with. For the others, we have made sure to think long and hard as to who should be present and then went and learned something about those people. It is quite normal for a team to focus exclusively on the presentation material and ignore the personalities to whom the presentation is directed. That is a big mistake. It is very important to figure out in advance whether your audience is one who prefers short bullets or detailed explanations, one that expects a lot of supporting data or one that looks to you for *your* opinion.

Having understood your audience, the next tip is to anticipate some of their concerns. For example, if the key stakeholder is the Financial Controller, you can bet that there will be concern about the amount of cash flow required for investment needed to execute a strategy. If it is someone from Quality Control, any attempt to reduce cost by compromising on quality will be thwarted. Likewise, if it is a team from marketing, they will be most concerned about image, time to market, and customer relationships. Engineers are less interested in the monetary savings and more interested in protecting technology. Talk their language and you will have a better chance of executing your strategy. Talk "Greek" to them and you will find yourself without any supporters. It's probably an oxymoron, but this is called "good lawyering." A good lawyer anticipates what her opponent will do in cross-examination of her client and tries as best she can to address some of those issues in her own examination. If possible she will show the jury that despite some shortcomings in her witness's testimony, the jury could still make the same conclusion. Thus, the opposing lawyer's thunder on cross-examination has literally been stolen. The same goes for your strategy. Think about what questions your audience will ask of you and try to address those questions in the appropriate section of your presentation.

Now prepare a presentation with the goal of "selling" the strategy to a targeted audience. The AIM & DRIVE Master Worksheet (Figure 8-5) is ideal for a brief presentation. In fact, the logic of the process is its strongest selling point. Few are interested in viewing every one of the worksheets. Those were to help the team put its thoughts down in writing. A short presentation from the Customer Service team of Anything Inc. would read something like this:

> "Ladies and Gentlemen, our team has taken the challenge of managing the cost of customer service at our company. Customer Service was chosen as a primary cost for our project team since we are running about 153 percent above budget and this is affecting the profitability of our company (**A**). Our team mapped the process and tracked various costs through the supply chain for this

service. Labor Costs at our supplier, Fixit, particularly the cost of their Technical Service and Field Service operators, were identified as the critical costs in this supply chain (**I**). Among many cost drivers (**M**) for labor costs, our team believes that the key cost drivers (**D**) are the Field Service efficiency, which is measured by the time taken to fix a problem at the customer site; the Technical Service Center efficiency, as measured by the number of field service trips required; and the Customer Service efficiency, which is measured by the number of phone calls transferred to the Technical Service Center. Numerous strategic options for each of these key drivers were put through a robust Risk-Benefit Analysis (**R**). Our team recommends that we increase the level of customer knowledge by creating "in-house" service technicians for major accounts. This should dramatically reduce the number of visits made by Fixit's field service technicians and save us about $3.68 million. We also recommend that there be a change in our replacement policy to allow Fixit to ship new/refurbished units to our customer via two-day service and have the customer ship defective units directly to Fixit's repair center. This is expected to save about $5.32 million over the next year. Our implementation plan (**I**) has been carefully laid out and we believe that these strategies and a couple of other minor ones will save our company around $14.5 million against the current expenditure of $23.2 million. We look forward to your support and participation in executing this strategy and are open to any questions you may have."

Who should make the presentation? Why is this important? In the many years that I have facilitated cost management strategy sessions I have witnessed many good, some great, and a few really poor presentations. In some cases I have seen team leaders spend most of their day on the phone or checking e-mail and hardly participating in the strategy-building session. Yet, when it comes time to present the
(*text continues on page 182*)

Figure 8-5. Master worksheet for customer service for goods under warranty.

AIM & DRIVE: Master Worksheet

Total Spend = $23,206,000

A PRIMARY COST : CUSTOMER SERVICE FOR GOODS UNDER WARRANTY

CRITICAL COSTS	COST DRIVERS	KEY COST DRIVERS	SELECTED STRATEGY STATEMENT	ACTION ITEMS	WHO	DUE DATE
I	M	D	R	I	VE	VE
Field Service Labor	FS labor rate FS efficiency TSC efficiency CS efficiency unit call rate	FS labor rate (# of hrs / visit call) FS efficiency	Increase level of customer knowledge by creating an "in-house" service technician for major accounts.	Identify key customers	Mktg	1-Jun
				Send rep to customer for preliminary meeting	Mktg	8-Jun
				Select target customer personnel for training	Mktg	15-Jun
				Perform in-house training	Mktg, Fixit	8-Jul
				Co-locate Fixit technician for trial run	Fixit	15-Jul
				Verify performance of in-house tech	Mktg, Fixit	8-Aug
		(# of visit calls / # of calls to TSC)		In-house tech performs repairs alone	Fixit in-house tech	15-Aug
Direct Material	unit price new part requirement repair effectiveness defect rate					
Freight	freight rate part weight shipment size	TSC efficiency (# of calls to TSC / # of calls to CS)	Change customer expectation to deal directly with TSC reps to ship replacements units directly to customers, and eliminate time limit policy.	Survey key customers and obtain feedback	Mktg	1-Jul
				Tabulate results	Mktg	8-Jul
				Confirm changes in freight and inventory costs	Mfg, Eng, Proc, Fin,	15-Jul
				Presentation to management	Mfg, Eng, Proc, Fin,	22-Jul
				Train TSC personnel	Fixit	10-Aug
				Implement new policy on shipping parts to customers	Mktg, Fixit	15-Aug

Objective	Task	Responsible	Date
Improve clarity of the service manual to increase customer's knowledge.	Analyze historic complaints to identify recurring problems	Eng, Fixit	15-Jun
	Red line current manual	Eng, QA, Mfg	28-Jun
	Prepare new manual	Eng, Fixit	28-Jul
	Print trial run and test with key customers	Mktg, Print	10-Aug
	Print trial version after any revisions	Eng, Fixit, Mktg, Adm, Print	17-Aug
	Distribute new manual to existing customers	Mktg	31-Aug
Increase the skill levels of CS operators to solve more problems over the telephone.	Analyze historic list of complaints to identify problems solvable over the phone by non-technical people	Eng, Mktg, Fixit	15-Jun
	Develop training program for CS operators	Mktg, Eng	30-Jun
	Train existing CS operators	Mktg, Eng	30-Jul
	Develop reference booklet of common questions and answers for CS operators	Mktg, Eng, Fixit, Adm	31-Aug

AIM & DRIVE strategy to top management, these same people are out there presenting on behalf of the team—and making a hash of it. It is extremely unprofessional for someone who presents to senior management to keep turning to the rest of his/her team for additional input, prompting, or to answer questions. I suggest, therefore, that the team select a spokesperson *at the beginning* of the AIM & DRIVE workshop. This person should be one who is comfortable speaking in front of an audience, a person who is articulate, speaks fairly rapidly, and has the confidence to field most questions. The reason I recommend that this person be chosen at the start of the strategy-building session is that it gives him/her time to think about what he/she is going to say. Knowing that you are the one to present will ensure that you ask questions if you have any doubts *while the strategy is being developed*.

Now, it's time to go out and implement your action plan. In the next chapter we will discuss how that plan can be verified with cost monitors so that you can experience the rewards of your efforts. It's payoff time.

Checklist for Step 6: Implementing an Action Plan

❑ Prepare a detailed list of actions for each strategy statement.

❑ Review risks from previous step and make sure to address those risks.

❑ Get agreement from all members of team on the action plan.

❑ Assign responsibility for each action item.

❑ Specify completion dates for each action item and get agreement from those who are responsible for each such step.

❑ Prepare a contingency plan.

❑ Identify audience for presentation of the strategy.

❑ Have the person presenting go through a rehearsal of the presentation.

❑ Make presentation to obtain buy-in for the plan.

Verifying the Plan with Cost Monitors

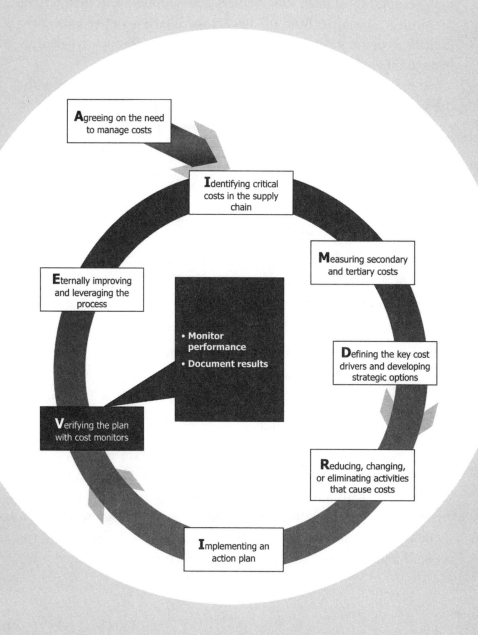

Having completed the implementation plan you might want to step back and bask in the glory of a job well done. Unfortunately, it is not done yet. All you have done is written a strategy and perhaps gotten the support needed to execute it. Nothing is worse than getting buy-in from stakeholders and suppliers and then letting the project slip. Apart from the likely loss of face it will be extremely difficult to get this support again. Yet teams have frequently failed to maintain the momentum.

At many of the companies that I have had the honor to work with, the key to success has been the development of a clear time line for executing the action plan and monitoring the savings or improvements. Here are some guidelines I have found useful for keeping teams focused and on target:

- Appoint a project coordinator.
- Hold regular team meetings.
- Attend all meetings.
- Avoid negotiations.
- Monitor ongoing performance.
- Document savings and qualitative benefits.
- Review Goals Specification Worksheet.
- Modify the action plan as necessary.

Appoint a Project Coordinator

It takes an official "nag" to make sure that the team stays on course and continues to execute the strategy that it spent so much time developing and writing up. This could be someone from the team or it could be an interested third party. Often, I've seen customers invite a member of the supplier team to lead the project execution. There is no hard-and-fast rule—except that the person must agree—and must have the time—to do it. The role of the project coordinator is to set up face-to-face meetings where necessary, although conference calls seem to be the norm these days. At companies like Motorola, one person was nominated as project coordinator for all AIM & DRIVE teams on the direct side and one for all indirect category teams. With conference calls virtually every day of the week with one category team or the other, and at the most unusual hours of the day to accommodate teams in the United States, China, Singapore, and Europe, I wondered when Motorola's project coordinator slept! But the effort paid off. Over a period of three years it was amazing to see over 300 strategy statements followed up for execution. How many companies could claim to have such a large number of ideas in the pipeline? Now, that does not mean that all 300-plus strategies were successfully completed. In some cases the teams went through the implementation process and realized halfway that the idea could not be implemented or that the product had been dropped. Still, it was a systematic approach to executing action plans. No one felt that they had wasted their time.

Nokia has a different culture but an equally effective one. There, category team leaders (they call them Supply Line Managers, or SLMs) were the project coordinators for their respective categories and were expected to manage the implementation process on their own. What I admire about Nokia is that when they see a good idea, they make quick decisions and execute the strategy with unbelievable speed. A lot of companies follow the same approach as Nokia, with category managers responsible for executing and managing the implementation plan. It really does not matter who is responsible for coordinating the project, just that someone is held responsible for it.

Hold Weekly or Biweekly Meetings or Conference Calls

Face-to-face communication among team members, whether in person or via conference call, is essential as the team proceeds to implement its action plans. How often, then, should the team meet? There is no standard answer to this question. In my opinion frequency should be based on the type of action plan that the team has written. Some action items may have a long time lag between activities and it makes no sense to meet every week when there is nothing happening. However, in most companies that I have been associated with, the recommendation to the team is that they meet once a week for the first three or four weeks and then once every two weeks for at least the next four or five months. Again, there is no fixed number of meetings but I've observed that teams that stay together for a six-month period have been able to document the best results. In some cases where my company has been asked to facilitate the follow-up of a strategy, teams have requested that we keep meeting once a month for another six months or so. They take on new projects and "live" the process of continuous improvement.

Attend All Meetings and Conference Calls—on Time, Every Time

Even though you are dealing with adults, and professional ones at that, it is necessary to emphasize the importance of being on time for conference calls and meetings. One supplier complained that certain category managers at a large utility company would set up conference calls at very inconvenient times for the supplier. Then, when the supplier's team called in, they had to wait for ages before the customer team showed up, if it showed up at all. In some cases it actually was just the supplier team and my representative. This is totally unacceptable. The customer should be represented on the call even if it is for a few minutes. At IBM, something similar happened with a category manager who invited a supplier from Minnesota to a face-to-face AIM & DRIVE meeting in San Jose and then pulled out of it himself at the last minute. I remember IBM's Director of Strategy and Procurement Processes personally apologizing to the supplier later. The category manager was removed from that position.

Avoid Getting Dragged into Negotiations

When teams meet on AIM & DRIVE projects it is important that the focus be on the collaborative effort to execute an action plan that they wrote earlier. However, it is human to forget that and fall into a "negotiation mode," especially when the action plan is not going as well as expected. It is very important that you not fall into this trap—and a terrible trap it is! A company I worked with in Germany had a disastrous experience with a supplier even though the initial strategy showed that there were potential savings of millions of euros. What happened was that the customer's representative who happened to be from Procurement could not draw the line between collaboration and negotiation. On every conference call he would bring in a totally unrelated issue, typically on component pricing. Even though we were working on a real breakthrough idea that could possibly reduce the price of an assembly by over 50 percent, the procurement person kept going back to the cost breakdown and the price of certain components. In spite of being advised over and over that this was not the place for negotiations, he would not let up. Ultimately the supplier called off its team and refused to participate any longer in the AIM & DRIVE initiative. It took a meeting between the Chief Procurement Officer of the customer company and the President of the supplier company to get the supplier team back to the table. The person from Procurement was removed from the team.

Monitoring Performance

The implementation of a plan in any project process needs to be monitored in order to make sure that action items are completed by a certain date. The project coordinator or team leader's job is to see that the worksheets are constantly updated. It is advisable to make notes that explain why a project plan, or any action item within it, is delayed. Not only does that help the team understand the cause of delay but those who may later use this strategy and its worksheets may learn from it as well. For example, the team may have had an unrealistic time line to implement an engineering change on a particular project. If another team, at a later date, is faced with a similar situation but in that case time is of the essence, they may think twice about going through with that decision. The Customer Service team at Anything Inc. used the worksheet in Figure 9-1 to monitor its performance against the implementation plan. The two other teams had a slightly different approach and offered comments on all action items. Some actions were completed on time. That was noted by the team. However, in cases where there was a delay, the teams made sure that an explanation was given. If strategies and implementation plans are to be leveraged, the more written comments there are, the better it is for others who may use this strategy as a base for their own. Observe the monitoring worksheets for Printed Manuals in Figure 9-2 and Corrugated Boxes in Figure 9-3.

As part of the monitoring process, it's good practice to develop a new process map showing the changes made as a result of the ideas implemented. Later, we will talk about maintaining a database of ideas. Having a sequence of process maps will allow others to see how the team progressed through the implementation of its strategy. A new process map is a graphic record that verifies that action has been completed and there have been activities that have been reduced, eliminated, or changed. Figure 9-4 shows a revised process map for the Customer Service team at Anything Inc. (The original process map can be found back in Chapter 4, in Figure 4-2.)

There are many ways to monitor performance. One way would be the old-fashioned process of having someone on the team keep an

(text continues on page 195)

Figure 9-1. Monitoring performance for customer service for goods under warranty.

AIM & DRIVE: Verifying the Plan

PRIMARY COST : CUSTOMER SERVICE FOR GOODS UNDER WARRANTY

SELECTED STRATEGY STATEMENT	ACTION ITEM	WHO	DUE DATE	COMPLETION DATE	COMMENTS
2 Increase level of customer knowledge by creating an "in-house" service technician for major accounts. Net Savings : $ 3,680,000	Identify key customers	Mktg	1-Jun	1-Jun	
	Send rep to customer for preliminary meeting	Mktg	8-Jun	8-Jun	
	Select target customer personnel for training	Mktg	15-Jun	15-Jun	
	Perform in-house training	Mktg, Fixit	8-Jul	8-Jul	
	Co-locate Fixit technician for trial run	Fixit	15-Jul	15-Jul	
	Verify performance of in-house tech	Mktg, Fixit	8-Aug	15-Aug	
	In-house tech performs repairs alone	Fixit in-house tech	15-Aug	22-Aug	
3 Change customer expectation to deal directly with TSC reps to ship replacements units directly to customers, and eliminate time limit policy. Net Savings : $ 5,320,000	Survey key customers and obtain feedback	Mktg	1-Jul	1-Jul	
	Tabulate results	Mktg	8-Jul	15-Jul	
	Confirm changes in freight and inventory costs	Mfg, Eng, Proc, Fin, Fixit	15-Jul	21-Jul	
	Presentation to management	Mfg, Eng, Proc, Fin, Fixit	22-Jul	28-Jul	
	Train TSC personnel	Fixit	10-Aug	25-Aug	
	Implement new policy on shipping parts to customers	Mktg, Fixit	15-Aug	31-Aug	
4 Improve clarity of the service manual to increase customer's knowledge Net Savings : $ 550,000	Analyze historic complaints to identify recurring problems	Eng, Fixit	15-Jun	15-Jun	
	Red line current manual	Eng, QA, Mfg	28-Jun	28-Jun	
	Prepare new manual	Eng, Fixit	28-Jul	8-Aug	
	Print trial run and test with key customers	Mktg, Print	10-Aug	17-Aug	
	Print trial version after any revisions	Eng, Fixit, Mktg, Adm, Print	17-Aug	24-Aug	
	Distribute new manual to existing customers	Mktg	31-Aug	8-Sep	
6 Increase the skill levels of CS operators to solve more problems over the telephone... Net Savings : $ 1,555,000	Analyze historic list of complaints to identify problems solvable over the phone by non-technical people	Eng, Mktg, Fixit	15-Jun	15-Jun	
	Develop training program for CS operators	Mktg, Eng	30-Jun	30-Jun	
	Train existing CS operators	Mktg, Eng	30-Jul	30-Jul	
	Develop reference booklet of common questions & answers for CS operators	Mktg, Eng, Fixit, Adm	31-Aug	31-Aug	

Figure 9-2. *Monitoring performance for printed manuals.*

AIM & DRIVE: Verifying the Plan				
PRIMARY COST : PRINTED MANUALS				
SELECTED STRATEGY STATEMENT	ACTION ITEM	WHO	DUE DATE	COMPLETION DATE	COMMENTS
	Customer survey to study impact on customer satisfaction	Marketing	21-Jun	21-Jun	Completed on time
	Determine number of manuals needed in hard copy	Marketing	28-Jun	28-Jun	Completed on time
	Prepare cost estimate of putting the manuals on-line	Mktg. / Proc. / Eng.	10-Jul	30-Jun	Completed ahead of schedule
	Make buy-in presentation to Paul Schultz	Mktg. / Proc. / Eng.	15-Jul	21-Jul	Paul Schultz not available
2 Print only the Quick Start Guide and have the rest of the manual available online.	If approved by Paul, redesign manuals to enhance graphics	Marketing	15-Sep	8-Oct	Delay mainly due to too many people having power to change design
	Design/develop Internet site	Mktg. / Eng.	31-Oct	15-Nov	Delay mainly due to too many people having power to change design
	Design troubleshooting guide for back panel of Zigmo	Mktg. / Eng. / Manuf.	31-Oct	31-Oct	Completed ahead of schedule
	Implement process changes to include the above	Manufacturing	30-Nov	30-Nov	Process implemented and tested. No bugs found.
	Implement "800" number for customer service	Marketing	30-Nov	30-Nov	Completed ahead of schedule. First year savings were documented at $5.7 million
Net Savings : $ 5,715,000					

Figure 9-3. Monitoring performance for corrugated boxes.

AIM & DRIVE: Verifying the Plan

PRIMARY COST : CORRUGATED BOXES

SELECTED STRATEGY STATEMENT	ACTION ITEM	WHO	DUE DATE	COMPLETION DATE	COMMENTS
1 Increase the # of pallet alternatives by eliminating pallets	Analysis of product list to see which ones the strategy can be applied on	Account manager	21-Jun	21-Jun	Completed on time
	Run pilot order with supplier on next Zigmo order without pallets	Account manager	28-Jul	10-Jul	Pilot order was delayed a week due to excess inventory
	Test different types of bubble wrap that can withstand forklift damage	Packaging engineer	10-Jul	10-Jul	Completed on time
	Evaluate and make Go /No Go decision	Packaging engineer	15-Jul	15-Jul	Completed on time
	If go, then execute across all shipments	Account manager	15-Aug	31-Aug	Pallet-less shipments were executed on 60% of the shipments but were held up on the rest due to resistance from other divisions
Net Savings : TBD					
3 Change type of middle liner from 26-lb performance to 23-lb performance	Gather samples of 23-lb. performance packaging	Procurement	28-Jun	28-Jun	Change of board weight approved beginning of Q4
	Meet with packaging engineers to review whether compression strength can be changed and that safety factor is realistic	Procurement	15-Jul	31-Jul	Delayed due to inavailability of engineers
	Establish minimum requirements; conduct compression tests	Packaging engineer	31-Jul	21-Aug	Compression test was delayed
	If tests are positive, initiate changeover process	Account manager	31-Aug	15-Sep	Changeover took place for 80% of product line
Net Savings : TBD					

Figure 9-4. New process map for customer service for goods under warranty.

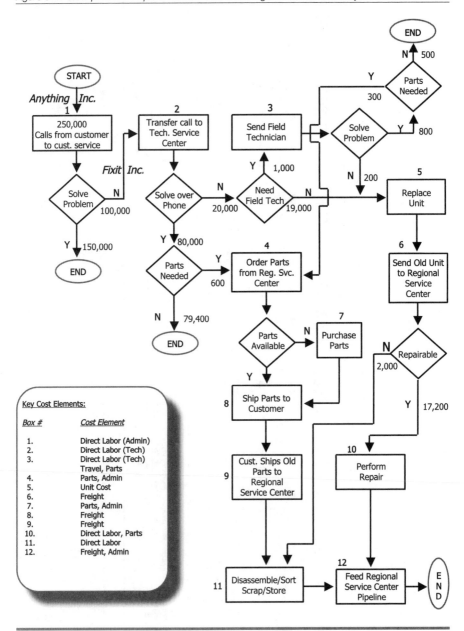

eye on due dates and remind the appropriate person that his or her action item is due. Today, with technology, a lot of this can be automated. With a basic software program an automatic message can be *pushed* to the person/s responsible for every action item. A computer program generates an e-mail to the members of a team, reminding them that an action item is due in a certain number of days. The lead time for such a notice is set by the project leader. If an action item is overdue by a certain number of days, a reminder is sent automatically to the responsible person. The project coordinator is copied as well. And, if the person responsible is delinquent by an unreasonably long time, the matter will be escalated to the appropriate level of management for further action. While this may seem like micromanaging it does get things done and that's what matters most.

Documenting Savings

Let's be honest. At the end of the day your management is not going to be happy unless you can show that your team has realized savings from your strategy. As strategies are completed it is important to document, to the best of your ability, the monetary savings as well as qualitative benefits from its execution. Figures 9-5 and 9-6 show how the Customer Services team at Anything Inc. documented its results and summarized them in the Verification Worksheet. It is particularly important when documenting savings that the team show how these savings were calculated. Notice the great detail showing where the numbers came from in Figure 9-5. Sometimes a lot of assumptions have to be made and the calculations will be difficult. In such cases, you must state the assumptions and make sure that at some point there is an effort to validate each one of them.

Documenting Qualitative Benefits

Not all strategies result in monetary benefits to the company. As you may have noticed in the risk-benefit analyses, there are some cases

(text continues on page 199)

Figure 9-5. Estimated savings for customer service cost for goods under warranty.

Details of Activities	Formula	Estimated Amount	Previous Amount	Difference (Savings)
1 250,000 calls to Customer Service Center (avg. 10 minutes per call @ $0.50 per minute)	(250,000 × 10 × $0.50)	$1,250,000	$300,000	$950,000
2 100,000 calls transferred to Fixit, Inc.'s Technical Service Center (TSC) @ 12 minutes per call. Service rate: $150/hour	(100,000 ÷ 5 × $150)	$3,000,000	$2,000,000	$1,000,000
3 Cost of parts needed for 600 calls solved by TSC @ $70 each	[600 × $(40 + 20 + 10)]	$42,000	$70,000	($28,000)
4 1,000 field service calls (avg. 2 hours per call @ $150/hour)	(1,000 × 2 × $150)	$300,000	$19,200,000	($18,900,000)

#	Description	Calculation			
5	Cost of parts needed for field service calls (80% of calls were solved of which 37.5% needed parts @ $70 each)	$(1000 \times 0.80 \times 0.375 \times \$70)$	$21,000	$196,000	($175,000)
6	Cost of defective units shipped back to Regional Service and repaired. 17,200 out of 19,200 repaired at a net cost of $200 each	$[17{,}200 \times \$(300 + 20 + 105 - 225)]$	$3,440,000	$806,400	$2,633,600
7	Cost of defective units shipped back to RSC that were scrapped. 2,000 units were scrapped at a net cost of $330	$[2{,}000 \times \$(300 + 20 + 10)]$	$660,000	$633,600	$26,400
	Total Cost of Customer Service for goods under warranty		$8,713,000	$23,206,000	($14,493,000)

Figure 9-6. Documenting results for customer service for goods under warranty.

AIM & DRIVE: Verifying the Plan

PRIMARY COST : CUSTOMER SERVICE FOR GOODS UNDER WARRANTY

	SELECTED STRATEGY STATEMENT	Net Expected Savings	Realized Savings [A]	Realized Expense [B]	Net Realized Savings [A] - [B]	Qualitative Results	Comments
2	Increase level of customer knowledge by creating an "in-house" service technician for major accounts.	$ 3,680,000	$ 3,030,000	$ 245,000	$ 2,785,000	Customer survey indicated significant increase in customer satisfaction thanks to faster turnaround	The actual reduction in field service visits was 21% lower than estimated
3	Change level of customer expectation to deal directly with TSC reps who will be authorized to ship replacement units directly to customers.	$ 5,320,000	$ 13,770,000	$ 3,995,000	$ 9,775,000	1. Same as above 2. Improved morale of TSC technicians	The actual reduction in field service visits was 20% higher than estimated
4	Improve clarity of the service manual to increase customer's knowledge.	$ 5,650,000	$ 180,000	$ 35,000	$ 145,000	Manual is more user-friendly	Manual usage was less than expected
6	Increase the skill levels of CS operators to solve more problems over the telephone.	$ 1,555,000	$ 1,920,000	$ 132,000	$ 1,788,000		
	Net Expected Savings = $ 16,205,000			Net Realized Savings =	$ 14,493,000		

where the team cannot quantify a benefit but it is listed nonetheless. For example, in virtually all strategic options that were chosen for implementation, one benefit is the increase in customer satisfaction. How would you quantify that? Yet, it is worth documenting if possible. If there is a way to show that the level of customer service, as measured by the number of complaints or by a survey of customers, has improved because of the execution of a strategy, then an effort must be made to conduct such a survey.

Review the Goals Specification Worksheet

I've noticed that many teams tend to get caught up with the execution of their strategies, most of which focus on cost savings. However, if you remember, back in the first step of the process where the team agreed to manage costs, they listed a number of goals from different perspectives. While verifying the action plan, it is worth taking a few minutes to revisit the goals for both Anything Inc. and Fixit and see whether progress has been made on most of those goals. Let's take a moment to list these goals again (see Figure 9-7).

With a savings of almost $14.5 million on the cost of customer service alone, Anything Inc. will be able to achieve its target profit margin of 5 percent. There are other goals besides the financial ones, both for Anything Inc. and for Fixit. For example:

- The new replacement policy provides a quick turnaround time thereby increasing customer satisfaction, which in turn should please Anything Inc.'s marketing team.
- With the introduction of in-house technicians the workload of the customer service center operations is reduced as fewer calls are made to the service center.
- Having a more knowledgeable customer at Anything Inc. will help Fixit achieve its goal of optimizing its technical service center workload.

Figure 9-7. Goals for customer service for goods under warranty.

AIM & DRIVE: Agreeing to Manage Costs	
Goals for Anything Inc.:	
Finance	Achieve a 5% profit margin
Marketing	Increase market share of Zigmos by 6%
Quality	Meet customer's product and service quality expectations
Procurement	Standardize parts for the Zigmo
Procurement	Obtain lowest Total Cost of Ownership of the customer service solution
Goals for Fixit, Inc.:	
Finance	Achieve a 7% profit margin
Marketing	Provide Anything Inc customers with world-class service with quick turnaround time
Logistics	Avoid shipment of parts by airfreight
Quality	Maintain high quality of repairs
Service Center	Optimize service center workload
Field Service	Maximize productive worktime

Modify Action Plans

During the verification phase of the AIM & DRIVE process it is important to go back to the analogy of a river. Be flexible and adapt to change. Sometimes when a team takes on a project at an AIM & DRIVE workshop, the right people may not be present despite the best intentions of both the customer and supplier companies. During the course of the workshop, certain strategic options are discussed, risks and benefits evaluated, and a strategy chosen for implementation. As the team continues to meet or conference over the next few weeks, certain issues or constraints may emerge that require the strategy or implementation plan to be modified. A team from a large telecommunication company was working with a supplier of key pads on an AIM & DRIVE exercise where it was decided to standardize the color on one of the keys. It seemed like a sensible thing to do at the time, especially since that action would result in savings of around $2 million. However, when we were a few weeks into the implementation plan someone from marketing joined in the conference call and was furious that the team had nearly completed the requalification of the key pad without consulting her group. Apparently there was a reason why that particular key had eight shades of red in the specification. While the strategy was not entirely dropped, the implementation plan had to be modified and the team decided to review the original specification, go out to the market, and conduct a new survey in different countries. They ultimately agreed, with Marketing on board, to reduce the number of shades from eight to two shades. It still saved about $1.6 million and saved the team a lot of embarrassment with the folks from Marketing.

Grading the Team

It is important to provide feedback to the team. At some companies I have joined senior management in grading the performance of teams that have implemented the AIM & DRIVE process. It's not just about the magnitude of savings. In many cases we grade the teams on how well they executed the process, the level of participation of the customer and supplier representatives, the leadership of the category manager, the drive or motivation of the entire team, and, yes, the amount of savings that was documented. There are times when it is important to show management that there was poor leadership or lack of participation from the customer company. Figure 9-8 is an example of a grade sheet on a group of AIM & DRIVE teams. Note the comments on the extreme right column.

Sharing the Learning Process

While documenting savings is important to the team and its management, sharing the AIM & DRIVE experience is equally important. At

Figure 9-8. Example of grading sheet for AIM & DRIVE.

Criteria for Grading Teams (A to F):			
1. Client participation. 2. Supplier participation. 3. Commodity Manager's leadership. 4. Drive/motivation to implement cost management strategies. 5. Documented savings			
TEAM (START DATE)	Individual Grades	Overall Grade	Issues/Comments
Sapura – Accessories (September 2006)	1. A 2. B 3. B 4. A 5. A (5%)	A	• This team has taken on three additional primary costs since it started and has realized savings for all of them • Good momentum
Augusta – Sensors (June 2007)	1. A 2. A 3. A 4. C 5. -	B	• This Cost Challenge has been slow so far compared to the Silverstone Cost Challenge (same MCD team) • 15% potential savings identified
Silverstone – Sensors (June 2007)	1. A 2. A 3. A 4. A 5. -	A	• This team has done a good job at getting engineering buy-in for the changes it proposes • 27% potential savings identified
Monza – Energy (November 2006)	1. C 2. B 3. C 4. C 5. A (16%)	C	• The strategies of this team are focusing on standardization but overall motivation is low • MCD realized 16% cost savings internally ("driving the usage of standard cells and standard packs")
Linear – Stabilizers (November 2006)	1. B 2. A 3. - 4. B 5. -	B	• This team is suffering from the lack of a commodity manager driving the effort on Syzygy's side • Good participation from the supplier • Great savings will be realized in 2008
POS – Stamping (August 2007)	1. B 2. A 3. A 4. A 5. -	B	• Good participation from the supplier and openness to change internal processes • Spend is too low to yield substantial savings

IBM, Gene Richter used to get the various category teams (IBM called them Commodity Councils) before his Procurement Executive Council (PEC) a couple of times a year. Commodity mangers were required to present their strategies and cost savings to Gene and his direct reports. I attended some of those meetings and what impressed me most was the candid feedback that was given to the commodity councils. Also, the fact that the other council leaders were present ensured that the learning of one became the learning of all.

In the next chapter we will take a look at how learning can and should be leveraged in order to maximize the impact of the AIM & DRIVE process.

Checklist for Step 7: Verifying the Plan with Cost Monitors

❏ Appoint a project coordinator.

❏ Hold weekly or biweekly meetings or conference calls.

❏ Attend all meetings.

❏ Avoid negotiating during AIM & DRIVE exercises.

❏ Monitor performance against action items.

❏ Draw a new process map.

❏ Document savings and show all calculations.

❏ Document qualitative benefits.

❏ Review goal specification worksheet.

❏ Modify action plan if necessary.

❏ Hold review sessions after six months to grade the team(s).

❏ Share the learning process by publicizing success and acknowledging development opportunities.

Eternally Improving and Leveraging the Process

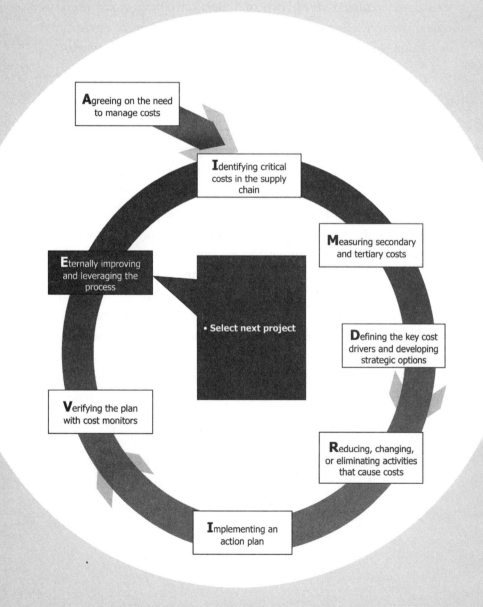

The journey of Cost Management, like that of Total Quality Management, never ends. I have yet to see a company that sends a message to its supply chain saying, "We are making too much money, please stop managing cost." Well, maybe you think that oil companies are in a position to say that. Think again. I work with three of the top five oil giants and believe me, there is an increasing pressure to manage costs. Not because they are concerned about eroding profits but because they realize that billions of dollars have been earmarked over the next five to ten years for capital equipment and more environmentally benign processes to extract and move oil around the world.

Expanding the Strategy

The AIM & DRIVE process is designed to continue the strategic focus on cost management, eternally. That's why I use the circle to demonstrate the process. By now you should understand that if you want to manage costs, not just cut them, you need to identify your critical costs, develop a list of cost drivers, pull out the key cost drivers, and develop strategic options for each of those. Then, you know that a strategy statement has to be written for selected options and a robust risk-benefit analysis performed in order to prioritize your options into strategies. After that, you must write a realistic implementation plan, along with a contingency plan. Lastly, you learned that it is important to verify both quantitative as well as qualitative benefits from the execution of the strategy. What next? Take a look at the circle, and there's your answer. Teams that I have worked with have taken the following basic steps to keep the AIM & DRIVE process alive at their respective companies.

1. Expand on the current strategy to fully exploit all the cost savings from a given strategy statement or statements. In the Customer Service example at Anything Inc., one of the biggest

savings came from creating in-house service technicians at key customer sites. The team could expand the number of companies where in-house service technicians are trained, thereby expanding that particular strategy to its full potential.

2. Select another strategic option for one of the key cost drivers, write a strategy statement, perform a risk-benefit analysis, write an implementation plan, and execute that plan. At Anything Inc., one of the key cost drivers was the Technical Service Center (TSC) efficiency (or inefficiency as in this case), as measured by the percentage of calls to the TSC that resulted in a field service representative being sent to a customer's site. A possible new strategic option would be to improve the communication skills of the TSC operators since it was noticed that in many cases they were not able to talk the customer through the solution even though it was a basic fix. The strategy statement would be, "Conduct communication skills training for selected employees in the TSC in order to increase the number of service calls solved by the Technical Service Center." Benefits would be fewer field visits, faster turnaround time, and increased customer satisfaction. Risks include the costs of selecting and training those who need better communication skills and the possibility that, once trained, a technician would leave the company to seek a job elsewhere. The implementation plan would include evaluating the technicians on communication skills, determining the right training program, selecting the trainer, conducting the training and evaluation, and then monitoring the results.

3. Select another key cost driver (or select a cost driver that was not earlier considered a key cost driver), list the strategic options, develop strategy statements for selected options, perform a risk-benefit analysis, write implementation and contingency plans, and then execute them.

4. Identify another cost element for the same primary cost or project, and run the rest of the steps for that cost.

You get the picture? It is an eternal circle of logic that can be applied over and over again. When it seems that you are scraping the bottom of the bucket, you may want to look at other projects that can use the AIM & DRIVE process to successfully take cost out of the supply chain. Pick another supplier or invite a customer to participate in a strategy writing exercise. Many suppliers that have attended my AIM & DRIVE workshops at the request of a customer have, in turn, asked me to help them apply the process with their internal teams as well as their supply base or with a customer of theirs. Can you imagine the look on the face of a customer when a supplier comes in saying, "We believe that we can work with you to take cost out of the supply chain? Here's a process and our commitment to work with your teams to implement the AIM & DRIVE methodology on this product/service we provide you. A large part of the savings will be passed on to you as a price reduction." The customer will probably fall off her chair in shock. But, think about the impact it would have made on your customer.

Finally, there are companies like Celestica who took what they learned from an AIM & DRIVE session with a customer and applied it to a number of their key suppliers.

Leveraging Ideas

It's been a long journey for many world-class teams that began with the oldest trick in the world: leveraging volume. Now, it's time to apply the latest best practice and that is to leverage *ideas* across the extended enterprise, that is, the "integrated supply chain." The strategy has to be expanded or leveraged in order to fulfill its potential. If I have ever seen lost opportunity, it is in this area. Ideas that could be leveraged but are not represent an unnecessary cost to the company. Here are a few ways to ensure that ideas are leveraged across product platforms, service contracts, and capital equipment purchases.

1. Set up an AIM & DRIVE database where the worksheets from various teams are stored.
2. Provide an incentive for teams to reach out to others who could use their ideas.
3. Hold idea-sharing sessions.
4. Use Web 2.0 technology to enhance communication of breakthrough ideas.

Setting Up an AIM & DRIVE Database

Leveraging ideas is the ultimate measure of success in a supply chain. We hear companies talking about knowledge management and introducing fancy programs that cost millions of dollars. Personally, I believe that it is the content that is more important than the software that manages that content. Not to say that data should not be managed. It should be easily accessible to those who need it and in a format that is consistent. Every company has its own way of storing data but Figure 10-1 illustrates how we managed and organized the AIM & DRIVE strategies for a telecommunications manufacturer.

The only way to access the Website is through the company's intranet. So the customer company gets to determine who has access to this data. In most cases strategies are open to members of all teams and across categories. If, however, there is some really proprietary information in a particular strategy that the supplier did not want other teams within the customer company to share internally, then those files will be blocked from viewing by anyone other than the specific AIM & DRIVE team. Suppliers, in turn, are given access to only those specific worksheets that they had participated in developing.

Figure 10-1. AIM & DRIVE database.

What goes on the Web page of an AIM & DRIVE Cost Challenge is totally up to the company setting this up. Typically, users get to view how to prepare for a strategy-building session (see Figure 10-2), or how to select and invite suppliers to participate in one. They could use a standard letter (Figure 10-3) to invite their key suppliers and then add a personal touch to it. Electronic versions of the templates are included so that the teams can begin filling them in as they discuss the various steps of the process. This is the basis of what one could call "codification of knowledge." Like all other database management processes, there must be a project master or someone who is authorized to upload templates, worksheets, and other documentation. I've seen team leaders given the rights to upload and modify their respective worksheets.

Figure 10-2. Preparing for an AIM & DRIVE session

Preparing for an AIM & Drive® Workshop

Selecting topics
- ○ Select 3–4 projects for the workshop.
- ○ A project is a spend amount with a supplier that will be the "topic" of the strategy developed during the workshop.
- ○ A project may include any one of the following:
    - —a specific part number, subassembly, assembly, OR a service performed by the supplier
    - —a family of parts
    - —a spend category (e.g., logistics, order fulfillment)

    Note: It is important that each project represent a spend that you would consider significant and that is likely to continue in the future.

Selecting and inviting suppliers
- ○ For each project, identify the supplier company that you would like to collaborate with.
- ○ Criteria for supplier selection include, but are not limited to:
    - —supplier with the largest share of business
    - —supplier that is most likely to "collaborate"
    - —supplier that is likely to get a large share of the business in the near future
- ○ Send letter of invitation to suppliers

Determining participants
- ○ Identify and ensure participation of team members.

    Note: It is <u>CRITICAL</u> for an effective project to ensure that the "right" people from both your company and the supplier participate.
    The "right" people include those who possess an in-depth knowledge of the "processes" involved as well as those with decision-making authority. Each participant must be able to make a valuable contribution to the discussions during the working sessions.

- ○ A project team is cross functional in nature and may include one or more of the following:

From your company	From your supplier
—commodity manager	—account executive
—operations/production	—operations/production
—design engineering	—design/process engineering
—marketing	—finance/accounting
—other internal stakeholders	—quality

- ○ *During the working session, specific questions may arise that require the input of experts from customer or supplier. These people may need to be teleconferenced or brought into the meeting to resolve a specific issue.*

Workshop logistics checklist
- √ AIM & DRIVE book and workshop manuals
- √ 1 LCD projector (with cables) for the instructor to project from his laptop and a projection screen
- √ 1 electrical power strip
- √ 1–2 flip chart with marker pens
- √ Preferable seating layout: round tables to allow seating in project groups
- √ Breakout rooms for the working sessions
    - —each room should be equipped with 1 flip chart, marker pens, and masking tape

Figure 10-3. Sample invitation to suppliers to participate in AIM & DRIVE session.

27 September 2007

Mr. Adrian Mole
Hoi Polloi Inc
1313 Wisteria Lane
Richmond, KS 66067

Attention: Mr. Adrian Mole
            Vice President, Product Engineering & Marketing

Dear Adrian,

As you know, cost management has become a critical success factor for us at Anything, Inc. To meet our cost management targets, we also know that involving our KEY suppliers is critical. To that end, Anything, Inc is aggressively pursuing new approaches of integration with our key suppliers to enhance our total supply chain. By managing our costs and rooting out inefficiencies together, we will be able to establish a sustainable competitive advantage for both your company and ours, and position ourselves to succeed in an increasingly competitive market.

We will hold a series of workshops run by subject matter experts to facilitate a collaborative cost management program with our key suppliers and Category Management Teams. As one of our key suppliers we invite you to participate in one of these sessions.

This program is based on Anklesaria's AIM & DRIVE methodology, which will enable us to collaboratively develop, evaluate, and implement cost reduction (process improvement) ideas. AIM & DRIVE is a proven collaborative approach that has been successfully implemented at numerous world-class, Fortune 500 organizations. The process harnesses the inherent knowledge of our supply chain to develop win-win total cost solutions.

The program will be rolled out in the following four phases:

1. Overview/buy-in session: 1-hour teleconference to provide an overview of the program, the AIM & DRIVE process, the resource requirements, and to clarify any issues or concerns
2. Education session: 2-hour teleconference to educate participants on the AIM & DRIVE process, and to communicate pre-strategy development activities and next steps
3. Strategy development session: 1-day face-to-face meeting to develop cost management strategies
4. Implementation and verification of action plans: Periodic teleconferences to monitor performance, enhance strategies, and document results

Anything, Inc is pleased to be able to offer what we believe to be an excellent program to you, and we are confident that it will be a valuable use of your time and resources. Thank you in advance for your commitment and contributions to Anything, Inc. I look forward to your participation in the program.

Sincerely,

Rick Ponting
Senior Vice President, Procurement
Anything, Inc.

Enclosures:

As teams complete the worksheets, their strategies are uploaded to the Website under the respective category folder. Within each category, there would be a folder for each supplier and within that folder would be the various projects. After a face-to-face meeting at which the strategy is first written, teams may decide to continue the work remotely. At a teleconference, the existing worksheets can be opened by the team leader and as discussion takes place the various worksheets can be updated on-line and saved on the database. In addition to worksheets, the project coordinator will file minutes of the meetings and teleconferences, spreadsheets to document savings, announcements, drawings, new specifications, road maps, and any other information that could be used later to trace how decisions were made by the team. Remember, the objective is that the learning of one becomes the learning of many. Think of what you would want to see if you were to join a new category team midway through a project, or were part of a new team that wanted to leverage off the work of another team.

Provide an Incentive for Teams to Leverage Their Ideas

In spite of all efforts to build a user-friendly and informative database, some people find it hard to visit the strategies of other teams. Why would a team member from, say, a Liquid Crystal Display (LCD) or Printed Circuit Board (PCB) category team visit the strategy of the marketing print team? Yet there are lessons and ideas that they could leverage if they did. In one company, the marketing print team came up with a strategy to get better utilization from a large sheet of paper as that sheet was cut into specific sized pages. That idea was then used by the team in charge of PCBs in what they termed "better panel utilization." Not to be outdone, the LCD team used the very same idea to increase by 12 percent the utilization from a glass panel—and glass was one of the largest cost elements in the display.

Some companies provide a financial incentive to teams that proactively contact other teams to share an idea that could be leveraged. Or, if financial incentives are not possible, a team that proactively shares its strategies with others may claim a small part of the savings of the other team against their target cost savings for the year. Think about the example of the facilities maintenance team in Campinas, Brazil, whose idea saved $160,000 on a project but was leveraged across the world for a total savings of $85 million for the company. Surely, if they had been the ones to proactively share this with their colleagues across the world, they should be given some credit for doing so.

Hold Idea-Sharing Sessions

A good leader is one who can motivate his or her team to learn from other teams. One of my coauthors of *Zero Base Pricing*™, Warren Norquist, Vice President of Procurement at Polaroid Corporation, used to get his teams to meet once every month for a brown bag lunch. There was no agenda other than for teams to share any cost management strategies with their colleagues. Companies like Nokia take teams up to the freezing Arctic where, in the warmth of a sauna, teams share their experiences and success stories. It does not matter how ideas are shared but it does make a big difference when leaders organize events that encourage teams to come together, have some fun, but also share their successes and frustrations with their associates. Sometimes key suppliers are invited to share in the process experience (but not details of their strategy). They are an excellent source of constructive feedback to customer companies. Over dinner the evening before an AIM & DRIVE session, TI would invite a supplier who had been through the process to address the suppliers about to go through it. The objective was not to have the supplier share all the details of the costs and how they were managed but rather to share the experience and, yes, frustrations with the process. One thing I noticed that was common among the speeches I heard. The suppliers tended to list as one of their disappointments the fact that "we did not do this earlier."

As I said, ideas need not be restricted to breakthrough cost solutions. In some idea-sharing sessions we have learned how important it is to select the right project, invite the right supplier, get the right people, and have the right attitude.

Use Web 2.0 Technology to Enhance Communication of Breakthrough Ideas

With technology moving at the speed of lightning you must always be ready and prepared to use the latest technology to communicate success stories through the supply chain. At the time of writing this book, my friend and schoolmate, Sabeer Bhatia, founder of Hotmail, is launching a new company called Blogeverywhere.com. When I heard about the technology for the first time I did not know much about Web 2.0 or the power of blogging. The more I learn about these technologies the more I am convinced that they are of immense use in leveraging ideas through the supply chain.

I said earlier that even with the best knowledge management tools and Websites, few will make the effort to visit AIM & DRIVE projects other than their own. It's time to use technology that pushes ideas to potential beneficiaries of those ideas. E-mail is outdated as a medium of communication between groups. Today, with technology like Blog everywhere.com, RSS (Really Simple Syndication) feeds provide a mechanism to allow automatic delivery of regularly changing content directly to a user's desktop. These feeds appear as a ticker on the toolbar of your browser. All it takes is for someone to be in charge of monitoring the AIM & DRIVE database and attach relevant strategies as a feed to potential teams that could use those strategies. What will happen is that if you are an authorized member of a cost management team, you would download the program (which is free) from Blog everywhere.com. Your name would be added to the AIM & DRIVE cost management list from your company. As and when the project coordinator thinks it fit to publish a strategy, those whose names are "tagged" as recipients will receive a small icon on a ticker that runs along the top of the toolbar. All you would do is position your mouse on the icon and it will summarize the topic or announcement. If you are interested in reading further you would double-click on the icon and it would pull up the AIM & DRIVE worksheet, memo, pod cast, notification, or whatever is being communicated and, presto, you are able to view or hear the idea. Even better, thanks to blogging capabilities, you can insert your own comment as a blog and read the comments of other members to whom this communication has been sent. I can see a day when suppliers are trained in the AIM & DRIVE process and will be asked to work on cost management strategies with their key suppliers, fill in the worksheets, and tag these as blogs intended for the category managers at their key customers for review and action if necessary. The world is getting smaller and flatter and anyone who shies away from technology does so at his or her own risk.

Critical Success Factors

Having seen AIM & DRIVE strategies applied at tens of companies over nearly seventeen years, it is clear that the success of a program like this depends on many factors. Here are a few tips on how to make this succeed at your company.

Success Factor #1: Top Management Support and Participation

There is no way around this. If top management is not willing to commit to a process of collaboration to achieve breakthrough cost solutions, you might as well not begin the effort. When I talk about support I do not mean lip service. A strong statement has to be made by the CEO, CFO, and the Chief Procurement Officer or Vice President of Supply Chain. This statement should be directed to the various stakeholders and category teams as well as to the supply base. Before launching the process at Texas Instruments, the Vice Chairman of the Board held a meeting of his key business unit heads in Dallas, Texas. They committed to doing their part in supporting the initiative. At IBM, Gene Richter made sure that either he or one of his direct reports kicked off every AIM & DRIVE workshop, even if it meant traveling halfway across the globe for just one day in order to show the stakeholders, teams, and, most importantly, IBM's suppliers that this process of collaboration meant a lot to Big Blue. Same thing at Motorola and TI. Some may consider this a waste of precious travel budgets but I can attest that the return on that investment was magnified a hundredfold.

Support of top management is a great start but their participation is even more vital to the success of a program like this. At Philips Semiconductors, the COO sat through the presentations of various teams after they had developed their respective strategies. He asked probing questions, challenged the teams to think outside the box, but always asked how he could help remove any roadblocks for them.

Success Factor #2: Supplier Top Management Commitment

When I talk about top management support, I should make clear that support must be obtained from the leadership of the suppliers as well. It is fine to have your own company's leadership involved but it is equally important that the suppliers see the value of a collaborative effort. There have been times when a supplier has sent an account representative alone to participate in an AIM & DRIVE workshop. That would be an indication that the supplier is participating only to please the customer and not to genuinely take cost out of the supply chain. Once, at Motorola, the AIM & DRIVE project leader canceled a session when he found out that none of the operations people from the supplier would be present, just three or four account managers. Later, a message went directly to the senior leadership and the session was rescheduled. This time the supplier was represented by top R&D engineers, manufacturing engineers, logistics experts, a person from finance, and, yes, the account representatives. Today, all agree that the project was a rousing success and their strategy is used as a benchmark for other teams. At Hewlett-Packard, the packaging category team would evaluate the commitment of the supplier based on who attended the AIM & DRIVE workshops.

Success Factor #3: Visits to Key Suppliers

In order to get the total commitment of key suppliers, especially those from other cultures, it is useful to send a senior representative from your company to visit with the supplier leadership prior to inviting them to an AIM & DRIVE workshop. Suppliers need to be assured that this is not another way of getting them to open up only to use that openness in the next negotiation. Texas Instruments sent its top managers to personally visit key Japanese suppliers before an AIM & DRIVE session. The purpose was to assure the suppliers that this was an important initiative for TI. It showed that TI valued the suppliers and would like to see them demonstrate support for the program by sending teams capable of suggesting ideas as well as with the power to execute them. I have never seen any company get such a level of openness and commitment from so many Japanese suppliers as Texas Instruments did in the 1990s.

Success Factor #4: Sharing of Cost Savings

A question that is commonly asked of me is, "How do customers and suppliers share in the cost savings from an AIM & DRIVE exercise?"

There is no standard answer to that. However, there must be some way of sharing in the spoils, otherwise why would a supplier participate in an initiative such as this? One way would be to split the documented savings in half and the supplier passes on the other half of the savings on its end to the customer in the form of a price reduction. In most cases it is not as easy as that. At times I have seen customers make a case for all savings to pass through to it in the form of a price reduction. This happens when the supplier's price is not competitive and the AIM & DRIVE process is used to help it become competitive, not through price negotiation but by genuinely taking cost out of its process. In another case, I remember working with a chemicals team at IBM with one of their major suppliers of chemicals and gases. IBM had squeezed the supplier's price down through negotiations in the previous year and the supplier was able to show IBM that it was, in fact, losing money on this account. Once the team validated the supplier's numbers, it determined that the first X amount of dollars of documented savings would go to the supplier in order to make them profitable again. Thereafter, the supplier would get 10 percent of incremental savings while IBM got 90 percent. You could not find a solution fairer than that. In this case, the supplier put in a sterling effort and IBM was able to realize a substantially lower price than the one previously negotiated because the savings well exceeded the initial dollar amount that was needed to bring the supplier back to profitability.

Measures of Success

AIM & DRIVE is about business process improvement. It is a strategic initiative and should not be used as a hammer to negotiate price at all cost. There are many nonquantifiable factors that need to be appreciated by a company's management. A lesson can be learned from the Total Quality Management process. A good quality program is one that focuses more on the process than on the measurable outcomes. That does not mean the outcome is not important. What it does mean is that if the process is robust and tested, the outcome will almost certainly be good. The same goes for the AIM & DRIVE process. If teams take on the challenge of developing breakthrough solutions and execute the AIM & DRIVE process in the manner that has been described throughout the book, success is virtually guaranteed. Instead of measuring only the documented cost savings a good leader would measure her teams based on:

- The percentage of total spend that has been covered by an AIM & DRIVE strategy
- The number of ideas that have been generated in those sessions
- The quality of ideas generated
- Documented savings from those ideas
- The number of ideas leveraged across other products or services managed by that team
- The number of ideas that were proactively leveraged to other teams
- The number of suppliers that have adapted AIM & DRIVE into their own processes
- The number of second- and third-tier suppliers that have been included in the process

Rewarding Success

Who does not like to be recognized or rewarded for a good effort? There must be a rewards program for teams, including suppliers, that perform well on an AIM & DRIVE cost management program. Some people would argue that the supplier's reward is the next purchase order. That may be true but how much does it cost to invite the leadership of the supplier company and present them with a plaque or certificate and say a few words of thanks? Not a lot—and it's the right thing to do.

Some companies are pretty innovative. Once, when I was doing a workshop for Texas Instruments in Singapore, I was told that we were going to have a longer lunch break that day. I dutifully ended the morning session around noon and was whisked away by car to the factory of a supplier nearby. There, we were taken to the cafeteria where a few hundred factory workers, all dressed in their work uniforms, were seated for lunch. To my pleasant surprise, the General Manager of TI, Singapore along with a bunch of other senior managers, including some of the supply chain leaders, personally served lunch to the workers. During lunch a few speeches were made, mostly thanking the operators for helping Texas Instruments meet their targets for cost, cycle time, quality, and delivery. A small gesture, but a very significant one indeed. Then we all joined in for some fun with a karaoke session. Yes, you guessed right. I sang Frank Sinatra's *My Way*.

Nothing works better than compensating teams with some monetary value for an outstanding job. There are companies that link a portion of a team's variable compensation to their performance and grade on an AIM & DRIVE initiative. I always advise those companies not to look at the total dollar values alone but to consider the percent savings as well. A pool of dollars can be set aside and shared between those teams that achieve or surpass their respective target cost savings, especially if those savings can be leveraged.

A more common way to recognize teams, especially the suppliers', is at a Suppliers Day. At such events, the senior leadership of selected suppliers is present to receive an award from the President or CEO of the customer company in front of other suppliers, stakeholders, and supply chain professionals. No money can pay for the pride that suppliers have when they are appreciated in front of others, especially some of their competitors.

*   *   *

Now it is time to go out and apply what you have learned from this book. Remember that you are not alone. You are part of a supply chain that has only one common objective—to delight the end customer with leading edge technology, world-class quality, on-time delivery, superior service, and all this at a lower cost than that of the competing supply chain. Good luck in your effort.

Checklist for Step 8: Eternally Improving and Leveraging the Strategy

❑ Expand on the current strategy to fully exploit all the cost savings.

❑ Select another strategic option for one of the key cost drivers and continue the process from there.

❑ Select another key cost driver or select a cost driver that was not earlier considered a key cost driver.

❑ Identify another cost element for the same primary cost and continue the process.

❑ Select another supplier or other project to implement an AIM & DRIVE strategy.

❑ Set up an AIM & DRIVE database to store all worksheets from various projects.

❑ Use Web 2.0 and other technology to spread the results and success stories.

❑ Leverage ideas across other similar product lines or service contracts.

❑ Reward participants for their effort in the process.

Index